Health Data Governance for the Digital Age

IMPLEMENTING THE OECD RECOMMENDATION ON HEALTH DATA GOVERNANCE

2016-2021

OECD

BETTER POLICIES FOR BETTER LIVES

This document, as well as any data and map included herein, are without prejudice to the status of or sovereignty over any territory, to the delimitation of international frontiers and boundaries and to the name of any territory, city or area.

The statistical data for Israel are supplied by and under the responsibility of the relevant Israeli authorities. The use of such data by the OECD is without prejudice to the status of the Golan Heights, East Jerusalem and Israeli settlements in the West Bank under the terms of international law.

Note by Turkey

The information in this document with reference to "Cyprus" relates to the southern part of the Island. There is no single authority representing both Turkish and Greek Cypriot people on the Island. Turkey recognises the Turkish Republic of Northern Cyprus (TRNC). Until a lasting and equitable solution is found within the context of the United Nations, Turkey shall preserve its position concerning the "Cyprus issue".

Note by all the European Union Member States of the OECD and the European Union

The Republic of Cyprus is recognised by all members of the United Nations with the exception of Turkey. The information in this document relates to the area under the effective control of the Government of the Republic of Cyprus.

Please cite this publication as:
OECD (2022), *Health Data Governance for the Digital Age: Implementing the OECD Recommendation on Health Data Governance*, OECD Publishing, Paris, https://doi.org/10.1787/68b60796-en.

ISBN 978-92-64-79752-9 (print)
ISBN 978-92-64-66055-7 (pdf)
ISBN 978-92-64-53443-8 (HTML)
ISBN 978-92-64-75621-2 (epub)

Foreword

OECD countries are increasingly concerned with having the right data infrastructure in place for producing health statistics and measuring health care quality and outcomes. This relates to information gathered through registries, administrative data, Electronic Health Records (EHRs), and other sources. It concerns data linkage between settings and levels of care, and mechanisms to generate and use timely, actionable data to support better clinical care and research.

Interest in strengthening health information systems has grown since the COVID-19 pandemic brought into sharp focus the importance of reliable, up-to-date information for decision making.

The Recommendation on Health Data Governance was adopted by the OECD Council on 13 December 2016. The Recommendation provides a roadmap for countries who adhere to it to achieve an integrated health information system that meets the health information needs of the Digital Age. Integrated health information systems support integrated health care delivery, high health system performance and value-based care, people centred health care services and world-class data environments for research and innovation.

All countries are encouraged to adhere to this Recommendation which provides guidance for building national governance frameworks that enable personal health data to be both protected and used towards public policy goals. The Recommendation:

- Encourages the availability and use of personal health data, to the extent that this enables significant improvements in health, health care quality and performance and, thereby, the development of healthy societies while, at the same time, continuing to promote and protect the fundamental values of privacy and individual liberties;
- Promotes the use of personal health data for health-related public policy objectives, while maintaining public trust and confidence that any risks to privacy and security are minimised and appropriately managed; and
- Supports greater harmonisation among the health data governance frameworks of Adherents so that more countries can benefit from statistical and research uses of data in which there is a public interest, and so that more countries can participate in multi-country statistical and research projects, while protecting privacy and data security.

This report documents progress among countries adhering to this Recommendation in its implementation from 2016 to 2021. It finds that countries are still in the process of implementing the Recommendation. Particular challenges to address concern harmonising approaches to data governance and to data standards to foster cross-country research collaborations and international benchmarking; and sharing best practices and supporting mutual learning to confront new cyber security threats.

Acknowledgements

This report was undertaken by the OECD Health Committee and its subsidiary bodies the Working Parties on Health Care Quality and Outcomes and Health Statistics and the Committee on Digital Economy Policy and its subsidiary body the Working Party on Data Governance and Privacy. The OECD would like to acknowledge the representatives from the countries who make up these working parties and committees who gave generously of their time to respond to surveys, to review drafts and to participate in workshops and meetings that lead to the completion of this report.

The contributions of the staff of the OECD Secretariat, in particular Jillian Oderkirk, Elettra Ronchi, Céline Folsché, Isabelle Vallard, Ricardo Sanchez Torres and Justine Deziel are also acknowledged. The authors would like to thank Stefano Scarpetta, Mark Pearson, and Francesca Colombo for reviewing this report.

Table of contents

FIGURES

TABLES

Follow OECD Publications on:

http://twitter.com/OECD_Pubs

http://www.facebook.com/OECDPublications

http://www.linkedin.com/groups/OECD-Publications-4645871

http://www.youtube.com/oecdilibrary

http://www.oecd.org/oecddirect/

Executive summary

The Recommendation on Health Data Governance was adopted by the OECD Council on 13 December 2016 on a proposal of the Health Committee (HC) and Committee on Digital Economy Policy (CDEP), and was welcomed by OECD Health Ministers at their meeting in Paris on 17 January 2017.

The Recommendation aims to guide countries adhering to it to set the framework conditions for enabling the availability and use of personal health data to unlock its potential. In so doing, it also provides a roadmap toward more harmonised approaches to health data governance across Adherents. The health sector remains significantly behind other economic sectors such as transportation, travel, banking and finance, in the interoperability of data. It was designed to be technology neutral and robust to the evolution of health data and health data technologies.

The Recommendation has provided important guidance to governments during the global COVID-19 pandemic. The pandemic shone a spotlight on the capacity of each countries' health information systems to provide critical information for the public welfare; as well as on aspects of data governance that created obstacles to responding to the pandemic in a timely way. Further, the Recommendation is a tool for the evaluation of countries' progress toward modern integrated health information systems that meet the information needs of the digital age and can support governments in times of crisis.

The need for an international standard on health data governance

Health data are necessary to improve the quality, safety and patient-centredness of health care services, to support scientific innovation, the discovery and evaluation of new treatments and to redesign and evaluate new models of health service delivery. The volume of personal health data in electronic form is already very large and is growing with technological progress including electronic health and administrative records; behavioural and environmental monitoring devices and apps; and bio-banking and genomic technologies. The scale, capabilities and methodologies of health data gathering, aggregation and analysis are also radically evolving.

When personal health data are linked and analysed, an exponential gain in information value can be attained to serve the health related public interest, such as improving diagnosis, particularly for rare diseases; identifying optimal responders to treatment and personalising care for better patient outcomes; detecting unsafe health care practices and treatments; rewarding high quality and efficient health care practices; detecting fraud and waste in the health care system; assessing the long-term effects of medical treatments; and discovering and evaluating new health care treatments and practices. Emerging technologies including Big Data analytics, for example, can utilise enhanced computing power to process broad ranges of data in real time, that, when applied to health can, improve patient-care and further the discovery of disease markers and disease-specific solutions.

However, often the data are held in silos by the organisations collecting them and there are uncertainties on how the potential benefits of the new analytic techniques can be achieved while ensuring the implementation of existing data protection standards and procedures. A 2013 OECD study showed that many OECD Members lack a co-ordinated public policy framework to guide health data use and sharing practices, so as to protect privacy, enable efficiencies, promote quality and foster innovative research.

There are benefits and risks from health data processing at both the individual and societal levels. The maintenance of a confidential health care system is fundamental to effective individual care and treatment, and to public health. Appropriate reconciliation of these risks and benefits is necessary to best serve the interests of both individuals and societies. In addition, international collaboration is essential to enable countries to safely benefit from health data and to support the production of multi-country statistics, research and other health-related uses of those data that serve the public interest.

It is against this backdrop that in 2014, the OECD Health Committee and the Committee on Digital Economy Policy agreed to jointly develop an OECD standard to tackle those issues – the Council Recommendation on Health Data Governance.

Scope of the Recommendation

The Recommendation applies to the access to, and the processing of, personal health data for health-related public interest purposes, such as improving health care quality, safety and responsiveness; reducing public health risks; discovering and evaluating new diagnostic tools and treatments to improve health outcomes; managing health care resources efficiently; contributing to the progress of science and medicine; improving public policy planning and evaluation; and improving patients' participation in and experiences of health care.

The Recommendation recommends that Adherents establish and implement a national health data governance framework to encourage the availability and use of personal health data to serve health-related public interest purposes while promoting the protection of privacy, personal health data and data security. Twelve principles set the parameters to encourage greater cross-country harmonisation among the health data governance frameworks of Adherents so that more countries can use health data for research, statistics and health care quality improvement.

The Recommendation also recommends that Adherents support trans-border co-operation in the processing of health data for purposes that serve the public interest. It further recommends that Adherents engage with relevant experts and organisations to develop mechanisms that enable the efficient exchange and interoperability of health data.

Finally, it encourages non-governmental organisations to follow the Recommendation when processing personal health data for health-related purposes that serve the public interest and invites non-Adherents to take account and to adhere to the Recommendation

Countries are still in the process of implementing the Recommendation

This report presents progress made by countries adhering to the Recommendation in implementing it and reports on its dissemination and continued relevance. It was prepared using three surveys (the 2019/20 Survey of Health Data Use and Governance, the 2021 Survey of Electronic Health Record Systems Development, Use and Governance, and the 2021 Survey of Health data and Governance Changes during the COVID-19 pandemic) as well as the results of several workshops including one on Health Innovation through Fair Information Processing Practices in 2021.

The 2022 Report confirms the continued relevance of the Recommendation, which has proven to be particularly important to address the COVID-19 pandemic. Overall, results indicate that there are many Adherents that are still working toward implementation of the Recommendation.

Among Adherents with lower scores for dataset availability, maturity and use, the challenge lies in making data available for research and statistical purposes. In these countries, there is work to be done to develop collaborative policies and practices among government authorities in custody of key health data. Considerable work and investments are required in such Adherents to improve data quality, linkability and sharing with researchers, so that data can serve health-related public interests. Among Adherents with lower scores for data governance, there are gaps to address in data privacy and security protections for key health datasets such as having a data protection officer and providing staff training, access controls, managing re-identification risks, and protecting data when they are linked and accessed.

The 2022 Report also concludes that the Recommendation has been widely disseminated to various stakeholders through various avenues, in particular through policy workshops, reports, scientific articles, newsletters and blogs and presentations to meetings and conferences. More work can be done and Adherents are encouraged to disseminate the Recommendation further at all level of governments and to non-governmental organisations.

Next steps

Over the next five years, the Health Committee and the Committee on Digital Economy Policy will continue developing tools to support the implementation and dissemination of the Recommendation.

Findings from this report are contributing to a new OECD Going Digital III horizontal project to support countries in strengthening data governance to support the development of digital societies.

Future work could focus on three areas that pose challenges for Adherents in implementing the Recommendation: 1) increasing the interoperability of health data and data analytics; 2) achieving greater harmonisation of health data governance frameworks for cross-country collaboration involving the sharing and use of health data; and 3) enhancing the sharing of experiences and best practices in health data security in response to the increasing occurrence of malicious attacks on health data.

1 Background

Health data are necessary to improve the quality, safety and patient-centredness of health care services, to support scientific innovation, to enable the discovery and evaluation of new treatments and to redesign and evaluate new models of health service delivery. The volume of personal health data in electronic form is already very large and is growing with technological progress including electronic health and administrative records; behavioural and environmental monitoring devices and apps; and bio-banking and genomic technologies. The scale, capabilities and methodologies of health data gathering, aggregation and analysis are also radically evolving.

When personal health data are linked and analysed, an exponential gain in information value can be attained to serve the health related public interest, such as improving diagnosis, particularly for rare diseases; identifying optimal responders to treatment and personalising care for better patient outcomes; detecting unsafe health care practices and treatments; rewarding high quality and efficient health care practices; detecting fraud and waste in the health care system; assessing the long-term effects of medical treatments; and discovering and evaluating new health care treatments and practices.

Emerging technologies including Big Data analytics, for example, can utilise enhanced computing power to process broad ranges of data in real time, that when applied to health can improve patient-care and further the discovery of disease markers and disease-specific solutions. Emerging technologies can also support and enhance privacy and data security.

Personal health data are sensitive in nature and fostering data sharing and use increases the risk of data loss or misuse that can bring personal, social and financial harms to individuals and can diminish public trust in health care providers and governments. Appropriate reconciliation of the risks and benefits associated with health data use is necessary if the interests of both individuals and societies are to be best served. This requires transparency, an understanding of the reasonable expectations of individuals and the development of a shared view of how best to serve the public interest in both the protection of health data privacy and in the benefits to individuals and to societies from health data availability and use.

OECD Initiative to Strengthen Health Information Infrastructure

The Working Party on Health Care Quality and Outcomes (HCQO) (and its predecessor the Health Care Quality Indicators (HCQI) Expert Group) has led an OECD initiative to support countries in strengthening their health information infrastructure since 2011. The impetus for this work was a call from OECD Health Ministers that was received in October 2010 to make more effective use of health data to improve health sector performance and quality of care.

By 2013, the Health Care Quality Indicators Expert Group (HCQI) (which became in 2017 the Working Party on Health Care Quality and Outcomes) [COM/DELSA/DSTI(2016)1/REV4] had published its first report on Strengthening Health Information Infrastructure (OECD, 2013[1]). The report documented a wide variation across surveyed countries in the development and use of health data. In particular, the study found that key health datasets in countries were often held in silos by the organisations collecting them and there were uncertainties about how the potential benefits of new analytic techniques could be achieved while ensuring the implementation of existing data protection standards and procedures. The report showed that many OECD Members lacked a co-ordinated public policy framework to guide health data use and sharing practices to protect privacy, enable efficiencies, promote quality and foster innovative research.

The report led to a follow-on study to continue monitoring progress in health information systems and to uncover and document promising health data governance practices (OECD, 2015[2]). The study, published in 2015, identified eight key health data governance mechanisms that maximise benefits to patients and to societies from the collection, linkage and analysis of health data while, at the same time, minimising risks to the privacy of patients and to the security of health data.

A second follow-on study, published in 2017, looked in-depth at the foundation of health information infrastructure, which is the development and use of data within electronic health record systems (Oderkirk, 2017[3]). The study found that countries are at very different stages of implementing and using EHRs, and that only a limited sub-group of countries have both strong technical and operational readiness to extract data from these systems for statistics and research, coupled with a health data governance framework and investments supporting data use.

The HCQO study results have been widely disseminated including within other OECD reports and academic literature exploring the development and impact of big data in societies, the development of health data governance principles, the impact of new health technologies and developing new analysis and research to advance care and treatment (Anderson and Oderkirk, 2015[4]; OECD, 2015[2]; Di Iorio, Carinci and Oderkirk, 2013[5]; Oderkirk, Ronchi and Klazinga, 2013[6]).

Development of the OECD Recommendation on Health Data Governance

The work of the OECD to support strengthening health data infrastructure and governance and to protect privacy and data security culminated in the OECD Recommendation on Health Data Governance [OECD/LEGAL/0433] (hereafter, the "Recommendation"), which provides guidance for building national governance frameworks that enable personal health data to be both protected and used towards public policy goals.

The studies described in the previous section were a catalyst for the development of the Recommendation, which was jointly developed by the Committee on Digital Economy Policy (CDEP) and the Health Committee (HC) with the advice of their respective relevant subsidiary bodies, the former Working Party on Security and Privacy in the Digital Economy (SPDE) (renamed since 2019 as the Working Party on Data Governance and Privacy) and the former Health Care Quality Indicators Expert Group (HCQI).

The development of the Recommendation also involved the advice of experts in privacy, law, ethics, health, government policy, research, statistics and Information Technology and extensive consultations with civil society (the Civil Society Advisory Committee, CSISAC) and business and industry (Business and Industry Advisory Committee, BIAC). The Recommendation was adopted by the OECD Council on 13 December 2016 [C(2016)176] and that was welcomed by OECD Health Ministers at their meeting in Paris on 17 January 2017 (OECD, 2019[7]; OECD, 2017[8]).

The Recommendation applies to the access to, and the processing of, personal health data for health-related public interest purposes, such as improving health care quality, safety and responsiveness; reducing public health risks; discovering and evaluating new diagnostic tools and treatments to improve health outcomes; managing health care resources efficiently; contributing to the progress of science and medicine; improving public policy planning and evaluation; and improving patients' participation in and experiences of health care.

The Recommendation recommends that Adherents establish and implement a national health data governance framework to encourage the availability and use of personal health data to serve health-related public interest purposes while promoting the protection of privacy, personal health data and data security.

National health data governance frameworks should provide for:

- Engagement and participation of stakeholders in the development of a national health data governance framework;
- Co-ordination within government and co-operation among organisations processing personal health data to encourage common data-related policies and standards;
- Reviews of the capacity of public sector health data systems to serve and protect public interests;
- Clear provision of information to individuals about the processing of their personal health data including notification of any significant data breach or misuse;
- The processing of personal health data by informed consent and appropriate alternatives;
- The implementation of review and approval procedures to process personal health data for research and other health-related public interest purposes;
- Transparency through public information about the purposes for processing of personal health data and approval criteria;
- Maximising the development and use of technology for data processing and data protection;
- Mechanisms to monitor and evaluate the impact of the national health data governance framework, including health data availability, policies and practices to manage privacy, protection of personal health data and digital security risks;
- Training and skills development of personal health data processors;
- Implementation of controls and safeguards within organisations processing personal health data including technological, physical and organisational measures designed to protect privacy and digital security; and
- Requiring that organisations processing personal health data demonstrate that they meet the expectations set out in the national health data governance framework.

These 12 principles set the parameters to encourage greater cross-country harmonisation among the health data governance frameworks of Adherents so that more countries can use health data for research, statistics and health care quality improvement.

The Recommendation also recommends that Adherents support trans-border co-operation in the processing of health data for purposes that serve the public interest. It further recommends that Adherents engage with relevant experts and organisations to develop mechanisms that enable the efficient exchange and interoperability of health data.

Finally, it encourages non-governmental organisations to follow the Recommendation when processing personal health data for health-related purposes that serve the public interest and invites non-Adherents to take account and to adhere to the Recommendation. As of the finalisation of this Report, no Non-Members have adhered to the Recommendation.

The Recommendation instructs the Health Committee, in co-operation with the Committee on Digital Economy Policy, to serve as a forum to exchange information on progress and experiences with respect to the implementation of this Recommendation, and to monitor the implementation of this Recommendation and report to the Council within five years of its adoption. The present Report aims at fulfilling the Council's instructions.

Methodology

To monitor the implementation, dissemination and continued relevance of the Recommendation, the Health Care Quality and Outcomes Working Party undertook three surveys: the 2019/20 Survey of Health Data Use and Governance, the 2021 Survey of Electronic Health Record Systems Development, Use and Governance, and the 2021 Survey of Health data and Governance Changes during the COVID-19 pandemic.

The *2019/20 Survey of Health Data Development, Use and Governance* measured elements of national health data governance including the implementation of national health data governance frameworks and related regulations and policies. The survey included a detailed review of data development, quality, accessibility, sharing and data security and privacy protections among the custodians of 13 key national health datasets. HCQO delegates, who are officials of health ministries or national health data authorities, co-ordinated the completion of the questionnaire within each of their respective countries.[1] Co-ordination of the completion of the questionnaire was more challenging in countries with decentralised health systems. For example, in the United States responses have been provided by various divisions within the Department of Health and Human Services (HHS) and by the National Center for Health Statistics (NCHS) based on their portfolios and may not be reflective of the entirety of health data governance in the United States health system. Twenty-two Adherents participated in the 2019-20 survey: Australia, Austria, Belgium, Canada, the Czech Republic, Denmark, Germany, Estonia, Finland, France, Ireland, Israel, Japan, Korea, Latvia, Luxembourg, the Netherlands, Norway, Slovenia, Sweden, the United Kingdom (Scotland) and the United States. In addition, Singapore, which participates in work of the HCQO WP and in the CDEP, responded to this survey even though it is not an Adherent.

The OECD 2019-20 survey was completed by all respondents before the onset of the COVID-19 pandemic in early 2020. As a consequence of the pandemic, all respondents made improvements in health data to support monitoring and managing COVID-19. In July 2021, the OECD conducted a Survey of Health data and Governance Changes during the COVID-19 pandemic. This survey examined the state of health data availability, timeliness, access and sharing and the need for and benefits of improved and harmonised approaches to health data governance that were adopted since March 2020. HCQO delegates were responsible for co-ordinating the completion of the questionnaire in their respective countries. Twenty-one Adherents responded to this 2021 "COVID-19 Survey" including: Australia, Austria, Belgium, Costa Rica, the Czech Republic, Italy, Japan, Korea, Latvia, Lithuania, Luxembourg, the Netherlands, Norway, Poland, Portugal, Slovenia, Spain, Sweden, Turkey, the United Kingdom, and the United States.

The OECD also conducted a 20*21 Survey of Electronic Health Record System Development, Data Use and Governance* in February 2021 ("EHR Survey"). Electronic health record (EHR) systems were surveyed separately because they represent a highly relevant and relatively new source of data on patients' health care journeys and are often managed by different national ministries or agencies from those responsible for national health data. This 2021 survey followed up on a previous 2016 survey on the same topic and measured the governance of clinical data within EHR systems and the technical and operational readiness to utilise electronic clinical records for statistical and research purposes. HCQO delegates were responsible for co-ordinating the completion of the questionnaire in their respective countries. Respondents to the 2021 EHR survey were officials of health ministries or national authorities responsible for electronic health record systems. Twenty-six Adherents participated in this 2021 survey: Australia, Belgium, Canada, Costa Rica, the Czech Republic, Denmark, Estonia, Finland, Germany, Hungary, Iceland, Israel, Italy, Japan, Korea, Lithuania, Luxembourg, Mexico, the Netherlands, Norway, Portugal, Slovenia, Sweden, Switzerland, Turkey and the United States. In addition, the Russian Federation, which participates in work of the HCQO WP and CDEP, responded to this survey even though it is not an Adherent.

2 Process

At the Health Committee (HC) meeting of December 2017, delegates discussed key activities that would take place to develop the Report to Council on the implementation, dissemination and continued relevance of the Recommendation [COM/DELSA/DSTI(2017)1/REV1] and agreed upon a plan which included the 2019-20 HCQO Survey of Health Data Use and Governance, followed by the 2021 HCQO Survey of Electronic Health Record Systems Development, Use and Governance. The final proposed step in would be interviews in 2021 with national officials responsible for health data governance regarding progress toward implementation. This step was later replaced with a follow-up survey on changes to data and to governance frameworks as a result of the COVID-19 global pandemic.

Within this plan, the Committee on Digital Economy Policy (CDEP) contributed information to the Report regarding progress and developments in the protection of personal data privacy and security and on national data strategies that are relevant to making continued progress in the governance of health data.

HCQO delegates discussed the proposed draft questionnaire for the 2019-20 Survey of Health Data Use and Governance at their meeting of 8-9 November 2018 [DELSA/HEA/HCQ(2018)9]. They also broke into small groups to discuss the opportunities and challenges in developing national health data infrastructure and governance.

First results from the Survey of Health Data Use and Governance were presented to the Health Committee meeting of December 2019 [DELSA/HEA(2019)18]. These early findings showed strengths, weaknesses and challenges in the implementation of the Recommendation and encouraged Adherents who had not participated to take part in the survey in Winter 2020.

First results from the 2019-20 Survey were discussed during the May 2020 meeting of the HCQO and the delegates discussed the impact of the COVID-19 pandemic on the development of health data infrastructure and governance [DELSA/HEA/HCQ(2020)1]. Delegates discussed changes in health data availability and governance that increased the timeliness, availability and sharing of data for both managing the pandemic and for research into mitigation and treatment.

The HC and CDEP gathered insights into progress and challenges in the implementation of health data governance frameworks through an international workshop on Health Innovation through Fair Information Processing Practices that was undertaken in collaboration with the Israel Ministry of Health and the Israel Technology Policy Institute on 19-20 January 2021. Key findings from the workshop have been published (Magazanik, 2022[9]).

The Working Party on Data Governance and Privacy in the Digital Economy (WPDGP), with the support of the Global Privacy Assembly (GPA),[2] organised three workshops to discuss how governments have addressed the privacy and data governance challenges in their fight against the COVID-19 pandemic. The issues arising during COVID-19 were directly tied to underlying health data infrastructure and governance. The first workshop held in April 2020 focused on the exceptional surveillance and contact-tracing measures adopted by countries and related legal uncertainties on how to enable the collection, analysis, effective anonymisation and sharing of personal data. Workshops in September 2020 and June 2021 focused on lessons learned by governments and on specific data protection and privacy challenges raised by e.g. vaccination programmes and COVID-19 "travel passports". Key findings from the workshops will be published in an OECD Report in Q4 of 2021 [DSTI/CDEP/DGP(2021)12].

Following final reviews by the HC and the HCQO, the findings of the 2019-20 Survey was published in April 2021 (Oderkirk, 2021[10]). The HCQO survey monitoring the Development, Use and Governance of EHR systems was launched in March 2021 and was completed by all respondents in August 2021. Results of this survey will be published in an OECD report in Q2 of 2022.

The brief HCQO survey monitoring Health Data and Governance Changes since the COVID-19 pandemic launched in June 2021 and results were presented to the Q4 joint meeting of the Health Care Quality and Outcomes and Health Statistics Working Parties and then integrated into this report in October 2021.

Taking into account all of the results of the different surveys and tools mentioned above, a draft Report has been developed:

- A **the first draft** Report was discussed during the joint meeting of the Working Parties on Health Care Quality and Outcomes and Health Statistics on 5 October 2021.
- A **second draft Report** was discussed by the WPDGP at its 22 November 2021, by CDEP at its 1 December 2021 meeting and by the HC at its 2 December 2021 meeting.
- Following these discussions, written comments sent by the delegations were included in the **third draft Report** which was approved by the HC by written procedure on 15 January 2022 [COM/DELSA/DSTI(2021)1/REV2].
- Following approval, minor adjustments were made in the Report, at the request of one Member, to the description of its domestic situation. The HC has been informed of these adjustments ahead of the transmission to Council [COM/DELSA/DSTI(2021)1/FINAL].

The Report was noted and declassified by the OECD Council at its 23 February 2022 meeting. A link to the approved Report is included in the public webpage of the Recommendation on the online Compendium of OECD Legal Instruments. Furthermore, in order to support the implementation and dissemination of the Recommendation, a policy toolkit on health data governance will be developed using the key points from the Report and will be disseminated as part of the Going Digital Project series of policy toolkits. Aspects of this Report will also inform the Going Digital III Project on Data Governance reports in 2022 on Tangible Responses and Recovery from the COVID-19 Pandemic; on Data Stewardship, Access and Control; and the final report from this horizontal project on Data Governance. The conclusions of the Report will also inform future work of the HC to support greater resilience to public health crisis among health systems; as well as further work in future years to support Members in strengthening their health information systems and the governance of health data.

3 Dissemination

In the Recommendation, the Council invited the Secretary-General and Adherents (at all levels of government) to disseminate this Recommendation.

OECD Health Ministers welcomed the Recommendation at their meeting in Paris on 17 January 2017, along with a call that the OECD undertake further work to support member and partner countries to further build capacity in this important area (OECD, 2017[8]). The Secretariat informed the public about the health data governance recommendation Q1 of 2017 through the Health Committee's newsletter and its website page dedicated to health data governance; as well as an article in the OECD Observer (Oderkirk, 2018[11]).

Health Ministers launched the Knowledge-Based Health Systems (KBHS) project in 2017 to help countries to adapt their health systems to manage efficiently and effectively the vast amounts of clinical, administrative, and other types of data being generated on a daily basis, so that this information could be used to improve health systems performance. The Knowledge-Based Health Systems (KBHS) project examined how countries could govern health data to take the next steps of extracting valuable knowledge from health data, and use this knowledge to drive positive health system transformation.

The importance of implementing the Recommendation was emphasised within the key messages and findings of the KBHS project which were discussed by the Health Committee at their meeting of June 2019 [DELSA/HEA(2019)12]. The KBHS project findings were published in a report that was launched at a high-level meeting organised by the OECD and hosted by the Danish Government on 21 November 2019 in Copenhagen (OECD, 2019[12]). The high level meeting *Health in the 21st Century: Data, Policy and Digital Technology* involved health ministers and senior officials in a discussion of the policy and institutional settings needed to extract knowledge from electronic health data and power 21st Century health care systems.

The key findings of the KBHS project and the call for development of health data governance was published as a chapter of the Handbook on Global Health published by the WHO and Springer (Colombo, 2020[13]). The OECD also published a booklet introducing and presenting the Recommendation in the spring of 2019 (OECD, 2019[7]).

Further dissemination of the Recommendation to industry and academic communities was facilitated through publications in academic journals and reports on topics including the need for real world evidence to support the development and evaluation of pharmaceutical products (Eichler, 2019[14]); the need for systematic evaluation of health data governance performance (Di Iorio, 2019[15]); foundations of the development of artificial intelligence (Oliveira Hashiguchi, Slawomirski and Oderkirk, 2021[16]) and opportunities and challenges in blockchain technologies in health care (OECD, 2020[17]).

The HC and CDEP further disseminated the Recommendation and gathered insights into progress and challenges in the implementation of health data governance frameworks through an international workshop on *Health Innovation through Fair Information Processing Practices* that was undertaken in collaboration with the Israel Ministry of Health and the Israel Technology Policy Institute on 19-20 January 2021. Key findings and proceedings of the workshop have been published (Magazanik, 2022[9]).

Specific topics discussed at this workshop included:

- Significant national health data governance reforms implemented recently in countries, which included legal and operational reforms to strengthen health data governance.
- Safeguards for health data sharing to promote innovation while protecting people's privacy including ethical review, data de-identification, administrative, technical and contractual safeguards, and safeguarding cross-border data flows.
- Privacy-by-Design and state-of-the-art solutions for safeguarding digital health data against unauthorised access and use.
- Perspectives of individuals and communities on the rights and interests of individuals, communities and societies regarding data protection and health including discussion of consent and alternative legal basis for the secondary use of patient data for research.

The OECD published a working paper Survey Results: National Health Data Infrastructure and Governance in April 2021 (Oderkirk, 2021[10]) and results related to health data sharing were developed as a Going Digital Toolkit interactive indicator on Trust (OECD, 2021[18]). The comparative results supported countries in the self-evaluation of their own progress toward implementation.

The OECD also supported Members in managing new data privacy and security protection challenges that arose during the pandemic from new flows of health data (i.e. case counts, hospitalisations, deaths, availability of resources, travel and migration, vaccination) and new forms of health data (i.e. smartphone apps, digital vaccination certificates). This included policy briefs in the spring of 2020 on key topics including "Ensuring Data Privacy as we Battle COVID-19"; "Beyond Containment: Health System Responses to COVID-19 in the OECD" and "Tracking and Tracing COVID-19: Protecting Privacy and Data while using Apps and Biometrics" (OECD, 2020[19]).

The need for greater consensus among countries on data governance frameworks was amplified by the pandemic and the OECD has had the opportunity to discuss and disseminate the Recommendation with other international organisations who are seeking to develop principles, recommendations or guidelines related to health data governance.

The G7 Health Ministers at their meeting of June 2021 focussed on international collaboration in health data. In preparation for this meeting, the OECD shared information on the Recommendation and findings from our surveys to support their discussions. The OECD took part in the World Health Organization Global Summit on Health Data Governance in June 2021 which served to announce their plans to build consensus among countries regarding health data as a public good. OECD has taken part in meetings of the Health Data Collaborative which is a collaboration of countries and the WHO that are working toward the development of agreed global standards for health data interoperability. The OECD also supported work of the G20 Digital Health Taskforce in 2020 and contributed to its report: Report on Digital Health Interventions for Pandemic Management. The OECD has discussed the Recommendation with I-DAIR, a new international digital health and artificial intelligence research collaborative and with the Lancet and Financial Times Global Commission (Health Futures 2030). The OECD has also spoken about the Recommendation to health care, industry, government policy, and data standards groups and associations in formal meetings and workshops and in bilateral discussions.

The concerns and challenges facing countries in managing the COVID-19 pandemic led to the OECD launching a new series of country reviews of health information systems in January 2021 following a discussion of this review series at the October 2020 meeting of the HCQO Working Party [DELSA/HEA/HCQ/HS(2020)2]. The country review series employs the Recommendation as the conceptual framework for the evaluation of country performance and the operational, policy and regulatory reforms recommended by the OECD to reviewed countries are based on the Recommendation.

Specific examples of Adherents' dissemination include:

- The Netherlands' Ministry of Health, Welfare and Sport commissioned the OECD to initiate a review of its health information system in January 2021 and to provide interim policy recommendations in April 2021 to be able to be considered as part of the agenda of a new government. The focus of the review of the Netherlands is to gather evidence to make informed recommendations of legal, policy and operational reforms to develop an Integrated National Health Information System that supports the policy goals of integrated care delivery; integrated public health monitoring and management; and capitalising on recent innovations and fostering research and development in technologies and treatments. (OECD, 2022[20])

* The Korean Ministry of Health and Welfare commissioned the OECD to initiate a review of its health information system in June 2021. The focus of this review will be on developing the health information system needed to improve the performance of the health care system by developing the data need to measure, improve and incentivise health care efficiency, efficacy and equity.

The work undertaken toward the development of the Report and the approved Report itself will be further disseminated through the 2021-22 OECD Going Digital III project which focusses on data governance. In particular, Module 1 of this project which will be reporting on data stewardship, access, sharing and control across different sectors of the economy including the health sector. The project will disseminate examples of best practices as well as recommendations for policy reforms that support data governance.

The WPDGP, with the support of the Global Privacy Assembly (GPA), organised three workshops to discuss how governments have addressed the privacy and data governance challenges in their fight against the COVID-19 pandemic. These challenges were directly related to countries underlying health data infrastructure and governance frameworks. The first workshop was held in April 2020 and focused on the exceptional surveillance and contact-tracing measures adopted by countries and related legal uncertainties on how to enable the collection, analysis, effective anonymisation and sharing of personal data. Workshops in September 2020 and June 2021 focused on lessons learned by governments and on specific data protection and privacy challenges raised by e.g. vaccination programmes and COVID-19 "travel passports". Key findings from the workshops have been published in an OECD Report [DSTI/CDEP/DGP(2021)12].

4 Implementation

The Recommendation has three main building blocks. It calls on Adherents to:

- Implement national health data governance frameworks and it sets out 12 principles to follow when doing so;
- Support trans-border co-operation in the processing of health data for purposes that serve the health-related public interest; and
- Engage with relevant experts and organisations to develop mechanisms that enable the efficient exchange and interoperability of health data.

Recognising the role of non-governmental organisations, the Recommendation encourages them to follow its content when processing personal health data for health-related purposes that serve the public interest. Finally, in order to level the playing field, it invites non-Adherents to take account and to adhere to this Recommendation. To date there are no non-Members Adherents but two non-OECD Members (Singapore and the Russian Federation) responded to some of the surveys developed to support the Report.

This chapter reports on progress among Adherents in the implementation of each provision of the Recommendation.

First recommendation: National health data governance framework

The Recommendation recommends that Adherents establish and implement a national health data governance framework to encourage the availability and use of personal health data to serve health-related public interest purposes while promoting the protection of privacy, personal health data and data security. A national health data governance framework can encourage the availability and use of personal health data to serve health-related public interest purposes while promoting the protection of privacy, personal health data and data security. The Recommendation sets out key elements of the development and implementation of national health data governance frameworks. The elements encourage greater cross-country harmonisation of data governance frameworks so that more countries can use health data for research, statistics and health care quality improvement.

The 2019/20 Survey of Health Data and Governance measured implementation of national health data governance frameworks and related regulations and policies. The 23 respondents to the 2019/20 survey were officials of national health ministries or national health data authorities.

A national health data governance framework can encourage the availability and use of personal health data to serve health-related public interest purposes while promoting the protection of privacy, personal health data and data security. Overall, 17 of 23 respondents reported that a national health data governance framework is established or is being established (Table 4.1).

Most respondents reported health data falling under a national health data privacy legislation; other data used in health studies falling under a national privacy legislation; and certain health datasets or health data programmes falling under other legislations governing ministries, data collections or registries. Some countries have legislations at different levels of government. Overall, 21 of 23 respondents reported that a national law or regulation exists that speaks to the protection of health information privacy and/or to the protection and use of electronic clinical records.

European Union (EU) member states implement the European Union (EU) Data Protection Regulation (GDPR) [Regulation (EU) 2016/679 of the European Parliament and of the Council of 27 April 2016]. The GDPR places personal health data in a special category with the highest standards of protection. Compliance requires that personal health data are very well organised and portable. For example, organisations must have data systems that allow them to fulfil individuals' rights to access their own personal data, to rectify or restrict their processing and to request data portability from one organisation to another; as well as to assure data are correctly categorised and demonstrate compliance with the regulation. In addition to national privacy laws compliant with the GDPR, most EU member states reported other national legislations with provisions specific to the protection of health data; such as laws regarding patient rights, the collection and management of health information, the provision of medical care and health care organisations, electronic clinical record systems and health research.

Table 4.1. National health data governance elements

Respondent	A national health data governance framework is established or is being established	Public consultation has occurred or is planned about the elements of the national health data governance framework	National law or regulation exists that speaks to the protection of health information privacy and/or to the protection and use of electronic clinical records	A central authority for the approval of requests to process personal health data is established or planned
Australia	Yes	Yes	Yes	Yes
Austria	Yes	Yes	Yes	Yes
Belgium	No	No	Yes	Yes
Canada	Yes	Yes	No	No
Czech Republic	Yes	Yes	Yes	No
Denmark	Yes	No	Yes	Yes
Estonia	No	No	Yes	Yes
Finland	Yes	No	Yes	Yes
France	Yes	No[1]	Yes	Yes
Germany	Yes	No	Yes	No
Ireland	Yes	Yes	Yes	Yes
Israel	Yes	Yes	Yes	Yes
Japan	No	No	Yes	No
Korea	Yes	Yes	Yes	Yes
Latvia	Yes	Yes	Yes	Yes
Luxembourg	No	Yes	Yes	Yes
Netherlands	Yes	Yes	Yes	Yes
Norway	n.r.	n.r.	Yes	Yes
Singapore (non-Adherent)	No	Yes	Yes	No
Slovenia	Yes	Yes	Yes	Yes
Sweden	Yes	No	Yes	n.r.
United Kingdom (Scotland)	Yes	Yes	n.r.	Yes
United States	Yes	Yes	Yes	No
Total Yes	17	14	21	16

Note: Note: n.r.: not reported.
1. Mission of the Health Data Hub is to elaborate a citizens and patients charter in collaboration with patient associations.
Source: Oderkirk (2021[10]), "Survey Results: National Health Data Infrastructure and Governance", https://doi.org/10.1787/55d24b5d-en.

Six respondents reported that their health data governance framework is set out in law (Austria, the Czech Republic, Denmark, Finland, France, and Germany). In Austria, there are elements of data governance within legislation governing health telematics, documentation and research organisation. In the Czech Republic, the National Health Information System and its governance are defined in the *Act on Health Services*. Finland's health data governance framework is set out in legislation regarding digitisation and management of client and patient information as well as in regulations and guidelines of the health ministry (THL) (See Box 4.1). Health data governance requirements, including GDPR requirements, are set out in federal and state laws in Germany.

Box 4.1. Finland: FinData

Findata is authorised by law to support the secondary uses of health and social data in Finland for projects that contribute to the public interest. Findata is the only authority that can issue permits for the secondary use of health and social data when the data is compiled from more than one data custodian. Findata provides for the secure linkage and research access to publicly funded datasets and registries including the data holdings of the Finnish Institute for Health and Welfare (THL), the Social Insurance Institution of Finland (Kela), the Population Register Centre, the Finnish Centre for Pensions and Statistics Finland. From 2021, Findata will expand to include data within the national EHR system (Kanta).

Findata is a centralised system issuing permits and a one-stop shop for the secondary use of health and social care data in Finland. It grants data use permits when data are requested from multiple registries or from the private sector; collects, links and prepares the data; provides the data in a secure IT-environment for data users; offers electronic tools for data permit applications; offers a help desk for data users; and works in collaboration with the controllers of the data.

Findata is not a permanent data repository, but a hub in which the data flows. It exists to streamline and secure the secondary use of health and social care data for four main purposes: 1) enabling effective and safe processing and access to data; 2) enhancing data protection and security; 3) eliminating overlapping administrative burden; and 4) improving data quality.

The *Act on the Secondary Use of Health and Social Data* (enacted in May 2019) gives Findata the authority to grant secondary use for research within Finland. It is noteworthy that this is made possible due to Finland's personal identification code that remains unchanged throughout an individual's life and is the key to linking personal information from various registries.

As a rule, the data are always disclosed to Findata's secure operating environment. However, the Act empowers Findata to make the data available in another environment as well, if it is necessary for the research purpose. These other environments will be audited for compliance with the regulation.

Source: Magazanik (2022[9]), "Supporting Health Innovation With Fair Information Practice Principles: Key issues emerging from the OECD-Israel Workshop of 19-20 January 2021".

In France, principles of data governance are set out in an *Act on the Modernisation of the Health Care System* which unified the governance of administrative health data in the custody of three organisations and enabled dataset linkages and set out principles and procedures for data access. The 2019 *Act on the Organisation and Transformation of the Health System* broadened the definition of the national health data system to include additional datasets and their custodians and set out data sharing principles among these custodians. A Health Data Hub is defining the elements of shared data governance with stakeholders. The Health Data Hub (HDH) was launched in 2019 to support France in becoming a leader in Artificial Intelligence in health and to overcome barriers to the re-use of health data for research (See Box 4.2).

Box 4.2. France: Health Data Hub

The HDH is a public interest group that was authorised by law and funded by the government to expand upon the existing national health data system (SNDS) to encompass all existing databases concerning publicly funded health activities (e.g. hospital electronic health records warehouses, cohorts, and registries). HDH was built on the infrastructure of the SNDS, the French administrative health care database that covers 99% of the population. The HDH catalogue unifies a collection of pseudonymised databases which the HDH is authorised to make available for research.

HDH's primary goal is to support research and innovation in health and health care by providing a unique entry point for secure and privacy-protective data linkage services and access to health microdata for research projects that contribute to the public interest, while respecting patient rights and ensuring transparency with civil society. The second goal was to design a state-of-the-art platform at the highest level of security, offering data storage, computing, risk mitigation and analysis capabilities. Finally, the third goal was to create a documented data catalogue built in a progressive manner to make priority data known to the scientific community.

The legal reform that launched the HDH aims to allow better visibility of common data assets for the entire ecosystem and to harmonise data access rules. Access to data is regulated and is carried out with respect for the rights of individuals. There is no obligation to process health data in France within the technological platform of the HDH and it is still possible to conduct research in other partnerships. HDH has so far launched 27 pilot projects, 9 of them COVID-19 related, after HDH received a specific mandate to accommodate COVID-19 related projects.

Permanent access to the HDH is granted to health authorities by decree of the French Ministry of Health. Other research requests for data are submitted to the "access team" that conducts a scientific and ethical assessment. If the request is found eligible, it is sent to the independent Scientific and Ethical Committee (CESREES). CESREES verifies that the purpose of the study is relevant and of public interest, that the data requested are in line with the study objective and that the proposed methodology is robust. If found positive, the project is submitted for authorisation of the French Data Protection Authority.

HDH consults with civil society by carrying out studies and consultations on the relationship that citizens have with health data and on their perceptions, needs and expectations. This knowledge is necessary to orient and adapt public communications, and to evaluate them and ensure they are clear. HDH also contributes to the implementation of a "health data culture" by providing educational tools to enable citizens to understand the data and to learn how to use them and how to carry out projects with them. (CNIL).

Source: Magazanik (2022[9]), "Supporting Health Innovation With Fair Information Practice Principles: Key issues emerging from the OECD-Israel Workshop of 19-20 January 2021".

In the Netherlands, a National Health Information Council works on the development and sustainability of national health information and includes health care organisations and the Ministry of Health. The Council has four information system development goals: data to monitor the safety of prescription medicines; citizen access to their own medical data and the ability to link their own health and medical data; digitisation and exchange of data between health care professionals; and that data is recorded once and reused. A sub-group of the Council is the Community of Data Experts which advises the Council about the secondary use of health data for statistics, research and health and health care policy. Several laws include rules that make it mandatory to keep a medical record, to provide patients with digital access to their medical records and regarding system quality. A new framework law that passed the parliament in 2021 requires the electronic exchange of medical records among health care providers.

In Korea, the Ministry of Health established a health data governance framework in 2018 and set up a Health care Big Data Policy Deliberation Committee which is responsible for data development, use and dataset linkages. Latvia developed a Health System Performance Assessment Framework in 2019 (including health care quality, patient safety and efficiency indicators). Within this framework, principles and procedures for data provision, data linkage, health data protection and access to data for research are set out.

The United States Department of Health and Human Services published in 2020 a final rule to implement provisions of the *21st Century Cures Act* of 2016 to support the seamless and secure exchange and use of electronic health records (See Box 4.3). The rule aims to increase innovation and competition by giving patients and their health care providers secure access to health information; allowing more choice in care and treatment. A provision in the rule requires that patients can electronically access all of their electronic health information (both structured and unstructured data) at no cost and deters blocking authorised access to and exchange of data. It calls on the health care industry to adopt standardised application programming interfaces (APIs) to allow individuals to securely and easily access structured electronic clinical data using smartphone applications.

The Department of Health and Human Services and the Office of the National Co-ordinator for Health Information Technology are releasing a Trusted Exchange Framework and Common Agreement (TEFCA) which sets out principles, terms and conditions for a common agreement to enable nationwide exchange of electronic health information across disparate health information networks. When implemented, it will aim to ensure that health information networks, health care providers, health plans, individuals and other stakeholders can have secure access to their electronic health information when and where it is needed.

Box 4.3. United States: New rule promoting access to data

In the United States, each state manages their own public health reporting programs, and these practices are regulated by state law. Each individual hospital system may have their own network – which can include thousands of payor systems. This fragmentation impedes patients' access to their complete records, as well as the availability of health data for research. To address this, the Department of Health and Human Services (HHS) published in 2020 a final rule to implement provisions of the *21st Century Cures Act* of 2016 to support the seamless and secure exchange and use of electronic health records. The rule asks the health care industry to utilise Application Programming Interfaces (APIs) and to adopt the HL7 Fast Health care Interoperability Resources (FHIR) standard for health data exchange. Further, a Trusted Exchange and Common Agreement (TEFCA) sets out principles, terms and conditions to enable the nationwide exchange of electronic health information across disparate health information networks.

Standardisation of the data sources is required for health data to be exchanged across all networks, not just the major networks like Medicare. The Office of the National Co-ordinator for Health Information Technology (ONC) has introduced a United States Core Data for Interoperability Standard, that will be the content and vocabulary baseline for health data. This standard includes new data classes and data elements, such as provenance, clinical notes, paediatric vital signs, addresses, email addresses and phone numbers. These data pieces were not universally exchanged before – but are essential for patient matching and identifying risk factors. Leveraging this data allows better demographic information to be available to health care providers so that they can evaluate patients' risks and needs.

ONC has several pathways for public engagement and input into these data interoperability standards including a federal advisory committee made up of representatives from health care, health IT, and patient advocacy organisations. It publishes proposals for public comment and conducts targeted listening sessions with different groups. Finally, on the technical aspects, it works closely with the standards organisations which include public input and consensus- based balloting processes.

Generally, there isn't financial support to all stakeholders to invest in this, but there is some support for states to implement these capabilities in their networks. For health care providers, there was previously a programme that provided incentive payments for adoption of an electronic health record system, but there has not been new funding approved by Congress to continue support. However, there are requirements for hospital systems that are paid under the Medicare (National) programme to adopt and use technology that is certified to certain standards and functionalities. There is also a programme that requires the payers (the plans that administer Medicare and Medicaid) to build Application Programming Interfaces (APIs, as well to allow the data they hold to also be accessible. And finally, ONC requires technology developers, through a certification programme, to make this technology available to their customers.

Source: Magazanik (2022[9]), "Supporting Health Innovation With Fair Information Practice Principles: Key issues emerging from the OECD-Israel Workshop of 19-20 January 2021".

In Australia, governmental responsibility for national health datasets is shared between Federal and State/Territorial jurisdictions. At each level of government, there is a range of agencies with responsibility for specific datasets and there is no overarching health data governance framework. However, all jurisdictions have signed the 2020-25 National Health Reform Agreement which includes an action to scale up a national approach to data governance arrangements, structures and processes, to facilitate clear and efficient mechanisms for sharing and developing data in a sustainable, purpose-based and safe way. There is an Australian data governance framework for electronic clinical data exchanged as part of the My Health Record System. A Data Availability and Transparency Bill was introduced in 2020 to implement a scheme to authorise and regulate access to Australian Government data (See Box 4.4).

Box 4.4. Australia: Data Availability and Transparency Reform

Varying legislative requirements across the Commonwealth, States and Territories, particularly for privacy and permitted uses of data, have historically made data sharing more complex. Challenges to effective and efficient sharing and use of data are not limited to legislation. Technical, data availability and data quality challenges have affected the application of data from both new and well-established data assets to respond to the needs of the health system and the different needs Commonwealth, State and Territory data users.

The Office of the National Data Commissioner (ONDC) in Australia has been tasked with developing a new data sharing and release framework, and overseeing the integrity of data sharing and release activities of Australian Government agencies. The ONDC released its first guidance in 2019 – the Best Practice Guide to Applying Data Sharing Principles – which provides general guidance to assist agencies in adopting international best practices in data sharing.

The Australian Government introduced the *Data Availability and Transparency Bill 2020* (DAT Bill) into the Commonwealth Parliament in late 2020. Once passed, the Bill will establish a new scheme to safely share Australian Government data. To support the implementation of the new data sharing scheme, ONDC is establishing digital services (known as Dataplace) to manage: the accreditation process under the scheme; the submission of data requests to data custodians; and the negotiation, registration and management of data sharing agreements.

It is intended that Dataplace will eventually support the sharing of Australian Government data both under the new data sharing scheme and through other data sharing mechanisms.

The ONDC is also preparing to implement a Data Inventories Pilot Program to develop individual data inventories for Australian Government agencies using common standards and then to aggregate these inventories into an Australian Government Data Catalogue. The Pilot will initially cover about 20% of Australian Government entities. The Pilot will support greater transparency of government data holdings, facilitate data sharing and assist the Australian Government to respond quickly in emergencies.

An Intergovernmental Agreement on data sharing, agreed by the National Cabinet on 9 July 2021, committed the Commonwealth, State and Territory Governments to share public sector data (including health data) as a default position, where it can be done securely, safely, lawfully and ethically. The principles-based agreement recognises data as a shared national asset and aims to maximise the value of data to deliver outstanding policies and services for Australians. National effort will also be focussed on specific time-limited national priority data areas, under the Intergovernmental Agreement's National Data Sharing Work Program.

The 2020-25 Addendum to the National Health Reform Agreement has committed to a series of national action to enhance health data to enable long term health reform and harness data and analytics to drive meaningful improvements in the health system. This includes: establishing a national approach to govern the creation, access and sharing of data from all Australian Governments and progressing mechanisms and interoperable systems for secure and comprehensive integration of data across patient journeys.

Source: OECD Questionnaire on Health data and governance changes during the COVID-19 pandemic, 2021.

Ireland's Department of Health is currently working on a national health information strategy. In this strategy, Ireland is planning a National Health Observatory which would be authorised by law and include the development of a national health data governance framework.

In Israel, the responsibilities for national health data governance are under the Ministry of Health. Israel's government has been working on designing a policy framework for secondary use of health data for research to enable collaborative data research initiatives. This framework is not yet finalised. As a result of the COVID-19 pandemic, the government has been accelerating work toward data sharing and access.

The Government of Canada, together with provinces and territories, is leading the development of a Pan-Canadian Health Data Strategy to improve Canada's collection, sharing, and use of health data while protecting privacy (Canada, 2021). An Expert Advisory Group (EAG), established to provide advice and guidance on the Strategy, released a first report setting out a vision for health data in Canada and establishing a basis for developing a practical approach to strengthen Canada's Health Data Foundation. A second report highlights the broad actions needed to support Canada's Health Data Foundation.

Slovenia began developing a national health data governance framework in 2019. Luxembourg is planning a National Health Observatory which will be authorised by law and will support the development of a national health data governance framework. Belgium reported an intention to increase co-operation among several federal health administrations (Federal Public Service Health (FPS Health), RIZIV-INAMI, FAGG) regarding data policy.

The United Kingdom (Scotland) has an information governance framework for personal data, within which is a Public Benefit and Privacy Panel (PBPP) for health and social care data. The PBPP is a patient advocacy panel which scrutinises applications for access to NHS Scotland health data for secondary purposes with respect to the public benefit and privacy implications of proposed projects.

Challenges experienced in developing national health data governance

The 2019-20 Survey of Health Data Development, Use and Governance asked about challenges and difficulties countries were experiencing in the development of health data governance. Virtually all respondents reported experiencing one or more data governance or technical challenges at the national level (Table 4.2). The most commonly experienced challenges were legal restrictions or policy barriers to public authorities undertaking data linkages (17 countries); concerns with the quality of data that limit their usefulness (16 respondents); and legal restrictions or policy barriers to sharing data among public authorities (14 respondents). A group of respondents reported experiencing a high number of health data governance and technical challenges: Australia, Belgium, Canada, Germany, Ireland, Luxembourg and the Netherlands.

Table 4.2. Challenges to the development of national health data governance

Respondent	Legal or policy barriers to sharing data among public authorities	Legal or policy barriers to public authorities undertaking data linkages.	Legal or policy barriers to public authorities extracting data from electronic clinical records?	Legal or policy barriers to sharing de-identified data with university or non-profit research organisations in your country.	Legal or policy barriers to sharing de-identified data with a foreign government or a foreign researcher	Lack of person identifiers to link the data	Concerns with the quality of the data that limit their usefulness	Lack of resources or technical capacity to process data or make data accessible for research and statistics	Other challenges
Australia	Yes	Yes	Yes	No	No	Yes	Yes	Yes	No
Austria	Yes	Yes	No	No	n.r.	No	Yes	No	n.r.
Belgium	Yes	Yes	Yes	Yes	No	Yes	Yes	Yes	Yes
Canada	Yes	Yes	Yes	No	Yes	No	No	No	No
Czech Republic	Yes	Yes	No	No	No	No	Yes	No	No
Denmark	Yes	Yes	No	No	Yes	No	No	No	No
Estonia	No	No	No	No	No	No	Yes	Yes	n.r.
Finland	No	No	No	No	No	No	Yes	Yes	n.r.
France	No	Yes[1]	Yes	No	No	Yes	Yes	No	n.r.
Germany	n.r.	n.r.	Yes	Yes	Yes	Yes	Yes	No	No
Ireland	Yes	Yes	No	No	Yes	Yes	Yes	Yes	No
Israel	Yes	Yes	Yes	Yes	No	No	No	No	No
Japan	Yes	Yes	Yes	No	Yes	Yes	No	No	No
Korea	No	Yes	Yes	No	Yes	No	No	No	n.r.
Latvia	Yes	Yes	No	No	No	No	Yes	Yes	n.r.
Luxembourg	Yes	Yes	Yes	No	No	Yes	Yes	Yes	n.r.
Netherlands	Yes	Yes	Yes	Yes	No	Yes	Yes	Yes	Yes
Norway	n.r.	n.r.	n.r.	n.r.	n.r.	n.r.	n.r.	n.r.	n.r.
Singapore (non-Adherent)	No	No	No	No	No	No	Yes	Yes	No
Slovenia	Yes	Yes	No	No	No	No	No	No	No
Sweden	No	No	No	No	Yes	No	Yes	n.r.	n.r.
United Kingdom (Scotland)	Yes	Yes	No	No	No	No	No	No	No
United States	Yes	Yes	Yes	No	Yes	Yes	Yes	No	n.r.
Total Yes	15	17	11	5	8	10	16	10	3

Note: n.r. not reported.
1. Legal restrictions to dataset linkages were eased through legislation introduced in 2019.
Source: Oderkirk (2021[10]), "Survey Results: National Health Data Infrastructure and Governance", https://doi.org/10.1787/55d24b5d-en.

The following 12 principles are part of the first recommendation to establish and implement a national data governance framework.

Principle 1: Engagement and participation

This principle asks Adherents to provide for engagement and participation, notably through public consultation, of a wide range of stakeholders with a view to ensuring that the processing of personal health data under the national health data governance framework is consistent with societal values and the reasonable expectations of individuals. Through open and public dialogue about potential benefits, risks and risk mitigations it is possible to promote a balanced approach to the governance of personal health data within society.

In 2019/20, 14 of 23 respondents reported that a public consultation had taken place or was planned about the elements of a national health data governance framework (Table 4.1).

Australia reported undertaking a stakeholder and public consultation as part of the steps toward developing a Framework for the Secondary Use of My Health Record system data. The My Health Record system is a nation-wide electronic health record system that contains a summary of patients' health information (Oderkirk, 2017[3]).

Netherlands includes client and patient federations as members of the National Health Information Council. Further, an open public consultation takes place in the Netherlands to review documents presenting data governance concepts. Health data governance development in Korea includes participation of civil society organisations and patients' organisations in order to reflect diverse public opinions.

Israel reported a public consultation process regarding secondary use of health data of the Ministry of Health, Digital Israel Bureau and the Innovation Authority, using public conventions and public feedback through a website.

Slovenia gathers public input to its health data governance framework through an e-Democracy portal. Latvia has undertaken in 2018 and continued in 2019 presentations and discussions with health care professionals and researchers.

Canada reported an intention to consult the public and an effort that is underway to develop the best method to do so and to determine the areas upon which the consultation should focus. France reported that a mission of the Health Data Hub is to elaborate a Citizens and Patients Charter in collaboration with patients' associations. Ireland reported that a public consultation will take place on the draft health information strategy.

The Czech Republic reported that a new law on e-health is being prepared that will include a revision of the law governing the National Health Information System (NHIS). As part of the development of this legislation, the public will be consulted. Similarly, Austria, Finland, Luxembourg and Singapore reported that public consultations take place whenever a legal reform is planned.

The United States Department of Health and Human Services provided a long open public comment period on the rule to implement the provisions of the *21st Century Cures Act* to support seamless and secure access, exchange and use of electronic health records.

Principle 2: Co-ordination within government and promotion of co-operation

This principle asks Adherents to co-ordinate within government and to promote co-operation among organisations processing personal health data, whether within the public or private sectors. This includes encouraging common data elements and formats; quality assurance; data interoperability standards; and common policies that minimise barriers to data sharing.

Legal restrictions, policy facilitators and barriers s to sharing personal health data

Fifteen respondents in 2019/20 reported a legal restrictions or policy barrier to sharing data among public authorities (Table 4.2). In Australia, there was an inquiry by the Productivity Commission into the benefits and costs of options for improving data availability and use. The Inquiry report in 2017 identified barriers to data sharing and release; and unnecessarily complex processes for data access. On the 2021 EHR survey, Australia reported that the opt-out programme for the secondary use of data in the My Health Record system as well as the COVID-19 pandemic has slowed progress toward enabling secondary use of this data source.

Belgium reported difficulties in 2019-20 sharing data among federal public authorities; between public authorities at the federal and regional levels; and between public authorities and semi-public actors, such as health insurance providers. In 2021, Belgium reported that there are legal restrictions to the secondary use of data within electronic clinical records.

In Canada, there are legal restrictions to the disclosure of personal health information among provincial/territorial public authorities and between provincial authorities and federal authorities. On the 2021 EHR survey, Canada reported that there is no consensus to share data extracted from electronic clinical records for national statistics or research. A 2021 report identified multiple policy barriers in Canada to health data sharing and use (Canada, 2021[21]).

In the Czech Republic there are legal restrictions to data digitisation that may present barriers to data sharing among public authorities. On the 2021 EHR survey, the Czech Republic reported that there are legal limitations to the development of the electronic health record system and that there is little sharing and linkage of health data held by different public authorities. Hungary reported in 2021 that a new legislation authorising the secondary use of data within electronic clinical records is in development.

Estonia reported that data protection legislation makes linking and accessing different data sources a complicated, bureaucratic and time consuming process. In Israel, the committee evaluating proposals for the sharing of data among public authorities decline proposals of public authorities that are determined to insufficiently protect privacy. In Luxembourg, each occasion of data sharing among public authorities requires a specific confidentially agreement.

In Latvia and Slovenia, data sharing among public authorities can only take place if there is a legal basis for it and laws are developed on a case-by-case basis. In Ireland there is a *Data Sharing Act* that applies to public bodies, however it excludes sensitive personal data, including health data. The Netherlands reports that sharing data for the purpose of calculating indicators of health care outcomes by health care institution is often prohibited.

Italy reported on the 2021 EHR survey that secondary uses and extraction of patient data from the electronic health record system for administrative, clinical and biomedical research are possible provided patients give their informed consent. De-identified patient data may be shared among public authorities and the Health Ministry for national epidemiological and statistical purposes as framed by recently amended legislation (Law. 205/2021).

Japan reports that the *Act on the Protection of Personal Information* requires that sharing of individuals' health data only take place with the consent of the individual or after the data have been anonymously processed according to a rule set out in the Act. However, personal data may be shared without consent subject to a legal authorisation for the sharing.

The survey asked about sharing de-identified data with researchers for statistical and research projects within the public interest; such as academic and non-profit researchers within the country, and foreign academic, non-profit and government researchers. Four respondents (Belgium, Germany, Israel and the Netherlands) reported restrictions to sharing de-identified data for research purposes within the country and seven respondents (Canada, Denmark, Germany, Ireland, Japan, Korea and Sweden) reported restrictions to such sharing with a foreign academic, non-profit or public sector researcher (Table 4.2). Sharing de-identified health data for research purposes with academic and non-profit researchers in the European Economic Area is governed by the provisions of the *EU General Data Protection Regulation* (GDPR) that came into force in May 2018. Under this regulation, de-identified data may be considered personal data and subject to the regulation.

In Germany, sharing of de-identified data (data that are not considered anonymous) falls under data protection legislations at the federal and state levels as well as under state hospital laws. With respect to foreign researchers, approval depends on the regulation governing the data involved. A solution can be to form a research collaboration with a German institution. On the 2021 EHR survey, Germany further reported legal constraints due to heterogeneous state level legislation and interpretation by data protection authorities (17 state and one federal DPA) and that secondary use of health data was often only possible with informed consent.

In the Netherlands, the health system is highly fragmented with multiple data holders and there are uncertainties among them regarding EU GDPR requirements as they relate to sharing data (as was discussed in the previous section) and sharing de-identified data has become more restricted. Many datasets in the Netherlands are held by health care providers who are not always willing to share data. As in Germany, a solution for foreign researchers to access data in the Netherlands is to become part of a Dutch research team.

In Sweden, the sharing of data with foreign researchers depends upon whether the data protection legislation of the receiving country is considered adequate vis-à-vis the national legislation. As a result, in practice, it is easier for researchers within the EU to be approved access to data.

In Estonia, sharing data can be a lengthy and bureaucratic process, however, it is possible for both foreign and domestic applicants to be approved. Belgium follows the EU GDPR and does not distinguish between national and foreign research use, but applicants must fulfil all of the conditions of the Information Security Committee and be approved by the data holders. Approval may be granted for scientific studies but not for commercial purposes. In Belgium, there is no policy with respect to sharing data. In Ireland, provisions of the *Data Protection Act* deal with the transfer of data to a third country; however, concerns of individual organisations whose data would be involved may preclude data sharing with foreign researchers.

In Australia, researchers who demonstrate that their work has been approved by the appropriate ethics committee should be able to securely access de-identified data. However, approval processes can be complex and lengthy. If the researcher is in a foreign country, then the difficulty is ensuring that the data could not be re-identified. The *Privacy Act* of 1988 requires that an entity that releases an individual's personal health data is held accountable if the foreign researcher mishandles the data. Further, the regulatory framework for the MyHealth Record (electronic health records) prohibits data within the MHR from being shared or stored outside Australia.

In Canada, some provinces and territories prohibit, by law or policy, the disclosure of de-identified personal health data outside of Canada. This and other barriers in Canada limit the sharing of de-identified data with researchers – in particular for cross-border research projects. There is no legal basis to share data with a foreign researcher in Korea.

Initiatives to improve health data interoperability

Twenty-one respondents in 2021 reported implementing policies or projects to improve the interoperability of data within electronic health record systems (EHRs). Eighteen respondents are adopting the HL7 Fast Health care Interoperability (Resource) standard and a further two respondents are considering adoption. The HL7 FHIR standard supports web-based applications in health care as they exist for other sectors such as for e-commerce, banking, and travel booking; and utilises commonly used web development tools which allow for a larger pool of developers and faster development. Thirteen respondents are also adopting

SMART on FHIR standards (or similar) and a further four respondents are considering adopting SMART on FHIR. Substitutable Medical Applications and Reusable Technologies (SMART) is a standard used on top of FHIR to develop web-browser and mobile/smartphone apps that can be connected to/interact with any EHR system. For example, an app to assist patients with managing their medications or an app for secure communication with a health care provider.

Fifteen respondents reported developing public application programming interfaces (APIs) and an additional respondent is considering adopting this standard. Application programming interfaces (APIs) allow data sharing among different EHR software and Health Information Technologies, overcoming blockages to data interoperability.

Table 4.3. Interoperability standards

Respondent	Implementing policies or projects to improve EHR interoperability	Developing public application programming interfaces (APIs)	Adopting HL7 Fast Health care Interoperability Resource (FHIR) standard	Adopting SMART on FHIR standards
Australia	Yes	Yes	Yes	Yes
Belgium	Yes	Yes	Yes	Yes
Canada	Yes	Yes	Yes	No
Costa Rica	No	No	No	No
Czech Republic	Yes	n.r.	Yes	Yes
Denmark	Yes	Yes	Yes	No
Estonia	Yes	No	Yes	Yes
Finland	Yes	Yes[1]	Yes	Yes
Germany	n.r.	n.r.	n.r.	n.r.
Hungary	Yes	Yes	No	No
Iceland	Yes	Yes	Yes	No[2]
Israel	Yes	No	Yes	No[2]
Italy	Yes	No	Yes	No
Japan	Yes	No	No[2]	No[2]
Korea	Yes	Yes	Yes	Yes
Lithuania	Yes	No	Yes	Yes
Luxembourg	Yes	Yes	Yes	No
Mexico	n.r.	n.r.	n.r.	n.r.
Netherlands	Yes	Yes	Yes	Yes
Norway	Yes	Yes	Yes	Yes
Portugal	No	Yes	No	n.r.
Russian Federation (non-Adherent)	n.r.	n.r.	Yes	Yes
Slovenia	Yes	n.r.	No	n.r.
Sweden	Yes	Yes	Yes	Yes
Switzerland	Yes	No[2]	No[2]	No[2]
Turkey	No	Yes	No	Yes
United States	Yes	Yes	Yes	Yes
Total Yes	21	15	18	13

Notes: n.r. Not Reported // n.a. Not Applicable // d.k. Unknown.
1. May not be open (public).
2. In consideration for adoption.
Source: OECD 2021 Survey of Electronic Health Record System Development, Use and Governance.

In 2021, 20 of 27 respondents reported a national organisation responsible for setting standards for both clinical terminology and data exchange (electronic messaging) standards. Nonetheless, the legacy of fragmented deployment of EHRs has resulted in 11 respondents reporting clinical terminology standards are inconsistent among different networks or regions within their country. While this remains a significant problem, it has improved from 2016 when 20 respondents reported this issue.

Table 4.4 National organisation responsible for EHR infrastructure and its role in setting data standards

Respondent	National organisation with primary responsibility for national EHR infrastructure development	Name of the organisation	National organisation sets standards for clinical terminology in Electronic Health Records	National organisation set standards for electronic messaging
Australia	Yes	Australian Digital Health Agency (ADHA)	Yes	No
Belgium	Yes	eHealth Platform & FPS Health	Yes	Yes
Canada	Yes[1]	Canada Health Infoway and Canadian Institute for Health Information	Yes	Yes
Costa Rica	No		n.a	n.a
Czech Republic	Yes	Ministry of Health, Department of Informatics and Electronic Health care (ITEZ)	Yes	Yes
Denmark	Yes	Danish Health Data Authority	Yes	Yes
Estonia	Yes	Centre of Health and Welfare Information Systems	Yes	Yes
Finland	Yes	Social Insurance Institution (Kela)	Yes	Yes
Germany	Yes	Gematik GmbH	n.r.	n.r.
Hungary	Yes	Ministry of Health and Director General of National Hospitals (OKFO)	n.r.	n.r.
Iceland	Yes	Directorate of Health, National Centre for eHealth Unit	Yes	Yes
Israel	No	Ministry of Health	Yes	Yes
Italy	Yes	Ministry of Economy, SOGEI (in-house system integrator)	Yes	Yes
Japan	Yes	Health Insurance Claims Review and Reimbursement Services and All-Japan Federation of National Health Insurance Organisations	Yes	Yes
Korea	Yes	Korea Health Information Service (KHIS)	Yes	Yes
Lithuania	Yes	Ministry of Health and State Enterprise Centre of Registers	Yes	Yes
Luxembourg	Yes	Agence eSanté	Yes	Yes
Mexico	n.r.		n.r.	n.r.
Netherlands	Yes	n.r.	Yes	Yes
Norway	Yes	Norsk Helsenett	No	No
Portugal	Yes	SPMS (Shared Services for the Ministry of Health)	Yes	Yes

Respondent	National organisation with primary responsibility for national EHR infrastructure development	Name of the organisation	National organisation sets standards for clinical terminology in Electronic Health Records	National organisation set standards for electronic messaging
Russian Federation (non-Adherent)	Yes	Ministry of Health and Ministry of Digital Development, Communications and Mass Media	Yes	Yes
Slovenia	Yes	National Institute of Public Health (NIJZ)	Yes	Yes
Sweden	Yes and No[2]	Multiple agencies involved at national and regional levels	Yes	Yes
Switzerland	Yes	eHealth Suisse	Yes	Yes
Turkey	Yes	Ministry of Health	Yes	Yes
United States	No[3]	Department of Health and Human Services	Yes	Yes

Notes: n.r. Not Reported // n.a. Not Applicable // d.k. Unknown.
1. Development and implementation is managed by each jurisdiction.
2. Some aspects are co-ordinated between a few authorities.
3. US Department of Health and Human Services adopts national standards and regulates the certification of EHR products. Governance of the exchange infrastructure is currently being defined. May not be open (public).
Source: OECD 2021 Survey of Electronic Health Record System Development, Use and Governance.

There is no global consensus regarding which terminology standard should be used for key clinical terms. There are, however, a few international terminology standards that are used by a significant share of countries. In 2021, 18 respondents reported using the International Statistical Classification of Diseases and Related Health Problems, 10th Revision (ICD-10) for diagnostic terms; 16 respondents reported the Anatomical Therapeutic Chemical (ATC) Classification System for medication terms; 13 respondents reported the Logical Observation Identifiers Names and Codes (LOINC) for laboratory test terms; and 10 respondents reported DICOM standards for medical image terms. There remain key terms within clinical records, such as surgical procedures, vital signs, healthy behaviours, socio-economic status, clinically relevant cultural and psychosocial characteristics and patient reported outcomes and experiences, where there is no consensus among countries about which international standard could apply. Further, there are often local standards that have been adopted or, in some cases, these elements are not coded to a terminology standard (recorded as free text). These results for 2021 are a small improvement from 2016, as the number of respondents adopting the ICD-10 diagnostic terms and ATC medication terms has grown by a few countries.

Twelve respondents reported adopting the Systematized Nomenclature of Medicine-Clinical Terms (SNOMED CT) for at least one key term within their EHR. SNOMED CT is a comprehensive set of terminology standards covering key terms within EHR records. The cost of deployment; however, is a barrier to widespread adoption and the number of respondents is unchanged from 2016.

Principle 3: Capacity of public sector health data systems

Adherents are asked to review the capacity of public sector health data systems including data availability, quality, fitness-for-use, accessibility, and privacy and data security protections; and to review elements of data processing that are permitted for health system management, research, statistics or other purposes in the health-related public interest, particularly access to datasets, dataset transfers and the linkage of dataset records.

Data availability, maturity and use

Key national health datasets are widely available across the countries surveyed and significant investments are made in health and health care monitoring and research in all countries. Overall, the respondents with the strongest indicators of dataset availability, maturity and use in 2019/20 are Denmark, Korea, Sweden, Finland, and Latvia (Table 4.4 and Table A A.1).

Dataset availability, maturity and use includes eight elements: dataset availability, coverage, automation, timeliness, unique identification, coding, data linkage and regular reporting of indicators of health care quality and system performance.

The top half of respondents tended to report progress in dataset availability, maturity and use since 2013; while the lower half of respondents tended to report a drop in capability, with the exception of Japan, which is making clear progress.

The OECD has put a priority on supporting Members and non-Members in measuring quality in health care, strengthening health data governance, developing knowledge-based health systems, and advancing health statistics. Nonetheless, cross-country variability remained significant in 2019/20 and pointed to challenges not yet overcome (Table 4.4).

The results presented in this report reflect the health data systems in OECD Members just before the onset of the COVID-19 pandemic in March 2020. The pandemic has since heightened governments' attention upon the long-standing gaps in health data and health information systems that we describe here.

Eleven respondents reported having all or virtually all of the 13 key national health datasets included in this study: Australia, Austria, Denmark, Estonia, France, Korea, the Netherlands, Norway, Singapore, Sweden and the United Kingdom (Scotland). Only two national datasets, however, were available in all respondents: hospital in-patient data and population health survey data. The least available national dataset was a cardiovascular disease registry dataset, which is available in ten respondents.

Table 4.5. Key national health dataset availability, maturity and use, 2019-20

Respondent	% of key national health datasets available[1]	% of available health care datasets with coverage of 80% or more of the population	% of available health care datasets where data extracted automatically from electronic clinical or administrative records	% of available health datasets where the time between record creation and inclusion in the dataset is one week or less	% of available health datasets sharing the same unique patient ID	% of available health care datasets where standard codes are used for clinical terminology	% of available health datasets used to regularly report on health care quality or health system performance (published indicators)	% of available health datasets regularly linked for research, statistics and/or monitoring (indicators)	Sum
Australia	92%	100%	56%	17%	17%	78%	83%	67%	5.09
Austria	92%	100%	78%	0%	33%	89%	75%	42%	5.17
Belgium	69%	71%	86%	11%	22%	71%	78%	33%	4.42
Canada	85%	75%	75%	0%	64%	100%	91%	100%	5.89
Czech Republic	77%	100%	100%	0%	90%	100%	90%	60%	6.17
Denmark	100%	100%	100%	77%	100%	100%	100%	100%	7.77
Estonia	92%	89%	78%	50%	83%	100%	92%	25%	6.09
Finland	85%	100%	56%	36%	100%	100%	91%	100%	6.67
France	92%	78%	56%	8%	58%	100%	83%	67%	5.42
Germany	31%	100%	33%	0%	0%	100%	100%	0%	3.64
Ireland	77%	86%	29%	0%	0%	29%	0%	0%	2.20
Israel	85%	88%	100%	18%	64%	100%	100%	64%	6.18
Japan	85%	100%	75%	0%	45%	88%	27%	9%	4.29
Korea	92%	89%	89%	58%	100%	100%	92%	67%	6.87
Latvia	77%	88%	63%	80%	80%	100%	90%	70%	6.47
Luxembourg	77%	100%	71%	10%	70%	86%	100%	30%	5.44
Netherlands	92%	70%	100%	0%	75%	100%	83%	83%	6.04
Norway	100%	80%	90%	0%	77%	90%	85%	69%	5.91
Singapore (non-Adherent)	100%	80%	100%	0%	62%	90%	31%	31%	4.93
Slovenia	77%	100%	100%	0%	70%	100%	70%	60%	5.77
Sweden	92%	100%	100%	8%	92%	100%	100%	92%	6.84
United Kingdom (Scotland)	92%	100%	67%	0%	0%	78%	67%	17%	4.20
United States	54%[2]	33%	17%	0%	14%	67%	57%	57%	2.99

Note: The sum column is the sum of the preceding columns and the maximum is 8.

1.Thirteen national datasets including ten health care datasets (hospital in-patient, mental hospital in-patient, emergency health care, primary care, prescription medicines, cancer, diabetes, cardiovascular disease, mortality and formal long-term care); patient experiences survey, population health survey and population census/registry.

2. Includes health and health care datasets of the US NCHS. Participation of US hospitals in NCHS national hospital data is insufficient to produce national estimates.

Source: Oderkirk (2021[10]), "Survey Results: National Health Data Infrastructure and Governance", https://doi.org/10.1787/55d24b5d-en.

Concerns about the quality of data that limit their usefulness

Overall, 16 respondents to the 2019-20 survey reported that there are concerns about the quality of national data that limit their usefulness (Table 4.2). Respondents reported concerns with the quality of administrative data when they are used for purposes beyond their original intent (Latvia, Australia); as well as with the quality of data entered/coded by health care practitioners in electronic records, which has not yet been widely assessed (Australia, Estonia). There is a problem with the usability of data within medical records in France due to multiple software providers and a lack of data standards; there is also a problem of lack of structured data and use of free text data capture in health records (Austria, France). The lack of common data standards across provinces and territories in Canada and inconsistent application of standards are emerging issues.

In the United States, lack of data standards, inconsistent data formats and inaccuracies in demographic data across different data sets diminish the accuracy of dataset linkages. Patient identity matching across datasets is usually reliant on patient demographic data as record linkage uses technologies such as a master or community patient indices and deterministic and probabilistic linkage methods. Studies have found that errors in data matching often result from the quality of patient demographic data, where the quality issues arose when the data were first collected during the patient registration process.

Timeliness is an issue, as are a lack of quality control mechanisms and sanctions for poor quality data (Belgium). In the Netherlands, medical care data from medical specialists in hospitals and ambulatory settings is not timely due to a long delay in billing data and the coding system used by these providers is difficult to analyse. There are health care sectors (including general mental health care, long-term care and health care for children and youth) where datasets are not available, are incomplete or are missing diagnosis. Coverage of diagnosis in the registry of primary health care visit and the coverage of secondary diagnosis in hospital data are data quality concerns in Finland. There are concerns in Germany about the quality of cause of death information in mortality data.

In Ireland, there are more concerns about dataset governance than quality. The Health Information and Quality Authority (HIQA) has written several reviews of information practices in key health datasets and has found several issues of governance.[3]

Quality of national health care datasets

Focusing on ten national datasets that are directly related to health care,[4] this study probed elements of data quality including population coverage, coding of clinical terminology, extraction of data from electronic clinical records, and timeliness.

Most respondents' datasets cover 100% of the target population; however, there are important gaps in some cases. Data gaps must be closed to have a full understanding of health care provision and outcomes. The most common reason why national datasets are not covering the full population is because they are missing records for care provided by private sector providers and institutions or that are covered by private insurance.

Only seven respondents (Czech Republic, Denmark, Israel, the Netherlands, Singapore, Slovenia and Sweden) reported that all datasets rely to some extent on data extracted automatically from electronic clinical data and/or electronic insurance claims or billing data. In most respondents, available key national health care datasets have some mixture of data entry from paper records and data extracted automatically from electronic records. The benefits of automatic data extraction include improvements in timeliness of data capture, avoidance of costs associated with paper data capture, and minimisation of errors that occur from transcription of information.

Thirteen respondents reported that for all of their key health care datasets clinical terminology is coded by assigning standard codes using a classification system, such as coding diagnosis to an International Classification of Diseases (ICD) code or coding prescription medicines to an Anatomical Therapeutic Chemical Classification System (ATC) code. Fifteen respondents reported that the majority of their available key health care datasets included data that had been coded by a clinician, such as a physician or nurse. Thirteen respondents reported that most health care datasets were coded by a health care coding professional. In most respondents, both coding professionals and clinicians are doing the work of data coding within national datasets.

Reliance on electronic data, as well as upon clinical professionals for coding, have a positive impact upon the timeliness of data within key national datasets. Data that are available in real time or near real time open the possibility of monitoring health care quality and performance in time to detect and address issues as they are emerging, including a rapid detection and response to adverse events. Denmark, Estonia, Korea and Latvia stand out for having a very short time lapse, of one week or less, between when a data record is first created and when it is included in the national dataset used for analysis for all or most key national datasets.

The 2021 COVID-19 Survey, which measures changes to health data and governance as a result of the pandemic, indicates that timeliness is the area where countries have made the greatest improvement to national health data. For example, while only 2 countries had weekly mortality data in 2019/20, by September 2021, 8 countries were reporting daily mortality data and another 5 countries were reporting this data weekly. Timeliness gains were also made in national health care data, particularly hospitalisations data.

In 2019-20, respondents were, for the most part, not reporting the use of national health datasets for either clinical or managerial decision-making in real time. The exceptions are Canada, where the inter-RAI tool within long-term care data has algorithms applied to it to alert clinicians in real time to areas of intervention, such as the risk of falls; the Netherlands, where national diabetes registry data are included in a dashboard available to clinicians for clinical decision making; and Sweden, where regional components of the diabetes registry are used for clinical decision-making.

The COVID-19 pandemic changed the need for and use of timely data for decision making at all levels of health care systems for epidemiologic surveillance and management of health care (See Box 4.5).

Box 4.5. Examples of timely data for policy decision-making in response to COVID-19

The COVID-19 Pandemic required countries to develop near real-time data to make appropriate decisions to limit the spread of the infection and adequately respond to health care needs. Below are a few selected examples of changes made to data systems to support decision-making.

Norway's Bered'C19 is a new data lake that was created in April 2020, which collects daily data on hospitalisations (via the Norwegian Patient registry), primary care, and emergency care. It links the records across data sources in real-time, on an individual level by personal ID number. This data lake was authorised in the Health Preparedness Act. Linkage of data was possible before the pandemic, but the timeliness and rapid time (hours/days) from data in-the-house to information for government has been a huge advantage.

Italy developed a new integrated COVID-19 national surveillance system reporting daily updates and weekly assessment reports to all Regions and Autonomous Provinces for decision-making regarding the epidemic risk and of the resilience of health care services. Luxembourg developed a system to collect data on Long Term Care residents and personnel on a daily basis together with quality control mechanisms performed by the Health Directorate in collaboration with the facilities.

Australia established the Critical Health Resources Information System (CHRIS), a nationwide dashboard of Intensive Care Unit (ICU) activity in 2020 where all ICUs provide data twice daily and are immediately able to see patient numbers and resources available within every ICU in their region and also see an aggregate summary of all ICUs in Australia. Summary ICU statistics are available to administrators in all state and territory health departments, and to all patient transport and retrieval agencies.

In Japan, the Gathering Medical Information System (G-MIS) provides public health centres with information on all medical institutions that provide treatment for COVID-19 infection, including the status of hospital operations, hospital beds and ICUs, medical staff, the number of visitors and patients, the number of tests, and the availability of medical equipment (such as ventilators and ECMOs) and medical materials (such as masks and other PPE).

The United Kingdom developed a new SitRep project for decision making at the UK level and within regions. SitRep reports daily to stakeholders about bed capacity within all hospital sites, the critical care workforce and PPE, oxygen and ventilation usage and capacity. To collect more complex data on a live basis and to enable better supply chain management and distribution of equipment and consumables, the National Health Service (NHS) worked with a private company (Palantir) to develop tools to support operational workflows and stock management for PPE and Ventilators and eventually also to monitor vaccinations. For vaccinations, there are now live data flows providing hourly vaccination rates where person-level data are written back into the electronic health records of General Practitioners (GPs) providing a strong proof of concept that near-live data collection is possible on a national scale.

Israel's Ministry of Health developed a COVID-19 database that collects data daily on tests, vaccinations, hospitalisations, deaths and other relevant health data. It was created for decision-making and a summary of the data is shared publicly on a national interactive dashboard.

Source: OECD Questionnaire on Health data and governance changes during the COVID-19 pandemic, 2021.

Capacity for national dataset linkages

Record linkages enable the information value of individual datasets to grow, permitting connections between health care provided and the outcomes of that care over time; and permitting data within one dataset to be put into context with data from other sources. The 2019-20 survey examined a set of technical factors related to capacity for record linkages including availability of a unique ID that could be used to link datasets, identifying variables that might facilitate linkages, consistency of the use of unique IDs, and the regularity of conducting dataset linkages.

Only for four key national health datasets (hospital inpatient data, mental hospital inpatient data, mortality data and cancer registry data) do the majority of respondents report that the dataset contains a unique patient ID that could be used for record linkage and that the data are regularly linked for research, statistics or monitoring (indicators). Opportunities to gain additional information value from other key national datasets through record linkages appear to be not pursued in many respondents (Figure 4.1).

Seven respondents (Czech Republic, Finland, Israel, Korea, Norway, Singapore, and Sweden) report having a unique patient/person identifying number that could be used for record linkage that is included within 90% or more of their national health datasets. Fourteen respondents report having the same unique ID number within 60% or more of their national health datasets.

Probabilistic data linkages involving matching records on other identifying variables (such as name, sex, birth date, address) could be used for the linkage of the majority of national health datasets in 16 respondents. In only Australia and the United States, however, it was possible to link the majority of datasets via these other identifying variables, but not via a unique patient/person ID number.

Over half of respondents report that dataset linkages are conducted on a regular basis with most of their national health datasets (Australia, Canada, the Czech Republic, Denmark, Finland, France, Israel, Korea, Latvia, the Netherlands, Norway, Slovenia, Sweden and the United States[5]). In contrast, dataset linkages are conducted on a regular basis with a minority of national datasets in Austria, Belgium, Estonia, Japan, Luxembourg, Singapore and the United Kingdom (Scotland) and with no national datasets in Germany and Ireland.

There are indications within this study that different unique ID's are used among national health datasets in some countries. Unless there are ways to match across different ID's, then these differences will prevent the use of these ID's for dataset linkages. Respondents challenged with 50% or fewer of national health datasets sharing a common unique patient/person ID number include Australia, Austria, Belgium, Germany, Ireland, Japan, United Kingdom (Scotland) and the United States.

A contributing factor to whether or not dataset linkages are conducted regularly is the number of custodians of key national health data sets. Most respondents have 3 to 5 different organisations in custody of the 13 key health datasets studied. However, in Ireland and the Netherlands there are 9 different organisations in custody of key national datasets and in France there are 7 different organisations. These respondents would have considerably higher challenges integrating and linking data across the pathway of care than in other respondents, as laws and policies governing health data accessibility and sharing would need to be considered and applied across multiple organisations.

Figure 4.1. Percentage of key national health datasets available and regularly linked for monitoring and research

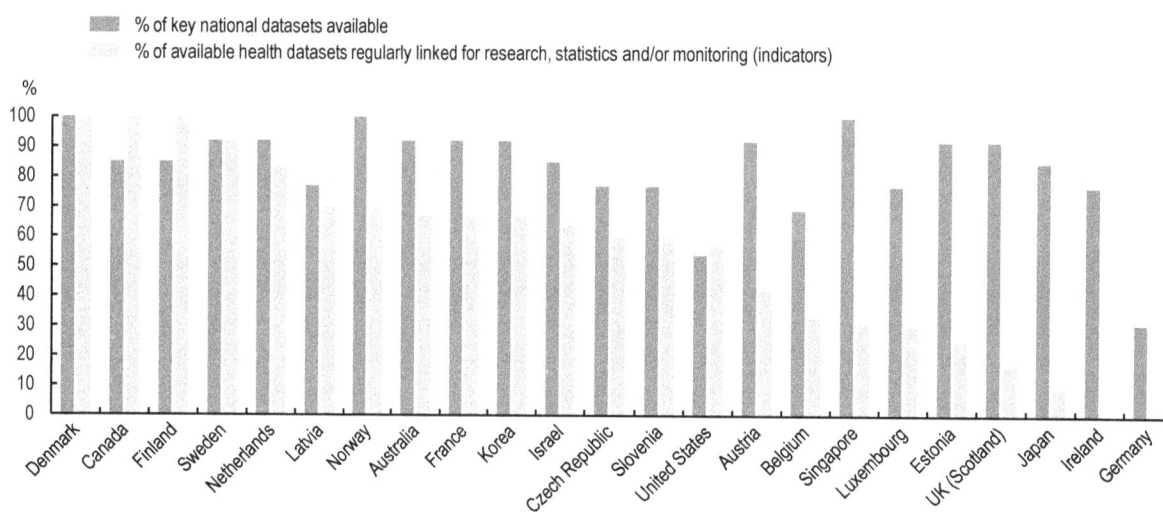

Source: Oderkirk (2021[10]), "Survey Results: National Health Data Infrastructure and Governance", https://doi.org/10.1787/55d24b5d-en.

Countries regularly linking data also shared insights into the purpose of these linkages that include: improving the quality of national information, such as validating data and filling in information gaps; providing new information about health care quality, outcomes, performance, accessibility and equity; and advancing epidemiological and health services research.

Eighteen respondents reported regularly linking datasets to monitor health care quality and/or health system performance. Examples of the types of indicators and analysis they undertake on a regular basis with linked data to monitor health care quality and/or health system performance include indicators of mortality at intervals after procedures, treatments or health care episodes; indicators of readmission to hospital; indicators of rates of prescribing medicines; and indicators of survival after diagnosis or treatment.

Legal restrictions, policy facilitators and barriers to dataset linkages

Sixteen Respondents in 2019-20 reported legal restrictions or policy barriers to public authorities undertaking dataset linkages. In Norway, there is no specific legal basis for dataset linkages. Similarly, there is no legislation in Japan that explicitly regulates the linkage of datasets of public authorities.

The United States *Health Insurance Portability and Accountability Act* (HIPAA) requires the creation of national identifiers for patients, providers, hospitals and payers; however, subsequent legislation prohibited the Department of Health and Human Services from funding the promulgation or adoption of a unique national patient identifier. Consequently, data matching is less accurate, poses patient safety risks and raises concerns regarding data integrity and compliance with any restrictions on data use authorised by individuals. Belgium also reports a lack of identifiers to track patients through care processes in different settings or levels of care.

In Canada, there are some provincial/territorial jurisdictions with legal restrictions or policy barriers to dataset linkages, particularly for the linkage of health and non-health data. Similarly, in the Czech Republic it isn't possible to link data within the National Health Information System to external data.

In Luxembourg, linkages among public authorities are difficult due to the provision of pseudonymisation services. In Slovenia, difficulties arise when the data to be linked are held in more than one public authority. In Israel, the committee evaluating proposals for the linkage of data among public authorities declines proposals determined to insufficiently protect privacy.

Legal or policy actions enabling access to and sharing of data among public authorities

Public authorities in Australia must be accredited as an Integrating Authority before they can undertake high-risk data integration projects, such as the record linkage of national (Commonwealth) datasets. Accreditation assures that the data integration will take place in a safe and secure manner.

In France, a new legislation in 2019 removed legal restrictions to the linkage of the national administrative health care (SNDS) dataset and other datasets governed by public authorities and set out conditions under which linked datasets can be created for multiple purposes.

In Korea, data set linkages among public authorities are legally possible but are limited in practice. The Big Data Platform Project aims to enable data linkages for health care research.

In Latvia, there must be a specific legal basis for a dataset linkage among public authorities to take place. In 2017, an agreement was signed among four public authorities (Centre for Disease Prevention and Control, National Health Service, State Emergency Medical Service and Health Inspectorate) to establish a linked health database to be used to fulfil a new framework for transparent indicators of health care quality, patient safety and efficiency.

Legal restrictions or policy barriers to public authorities extracting data from electronic health records

While many countries are extracting data from electronic clinical records to develop their key national datasets and for research, ten respondents in 2019-20 reported barriers to doing so.

In the Netherlands, there are problems that have arisen following the introduction of the EU GDPR. In the Netherlands, health datasets are in the custody of various public sector organisations (such as the Dutch Hospital Data institute, and the Perined (childbirth data) institute). Among the custodians of health data, there are different interpretations of the EU GDPR and some have determined that past data exchange arrangements are no longer legally permitted. To clarify that data exchange is lawful, some organisations and institutes are asking government for legislation authorising the exchange of electronic clinical data.

In Luxembourg, data extraction from electronic clinical records for secondary uses is only lawful with the prior written consent of patients. Similarly, in Canada, electronic medical records in primary health care are in the custody and control of care providers who have no obligation and sometimes, depending on the jurisdiction, no legal authority to share data with public authorities, without express consent. As in Canada, the federal structure of Germany leads to different legal frameworks at the state level (state data protection laws, state hospital laws) that govern whether or not data may be extracted for secondary purposes. In

Australia, data extraction is restricted by a number of legislative, privacy, secrecy and confidentiality requirements and medical records can be disclosed with consent, or in specified circumstances where authorised by law.

In France, there is a legal prohibition against extracting data from the electronic health record or DMP (dossier médical partagé) for the purposes of sharing and linking data as part of the health care information system modernisation effort. France reports the legal prohibition came about because the national health insurance fund (CNAM) provides operational management of the linked health care administrative database and patients' associations sought a guarantee that clinical data within the DMP would not be accessible to the insurer. It is, however, legally possible to create a dataset of anonymised data from DMP records.

In Japan, there is no national electronic health record system within which data might be contributed by each medical institution. Further, medical institutions require, in principle, patient consent for each research or statistical project where data would be extracted and shared from their electronic records.

In Belgium, there is no real policy about the extraction of data from electronic records for secondary uses. In Latvia, there is no experience yet with data extraction as the implementation of the national e-health system has only started recently. In Ireland, most health records remain paper-based in acute care hospitals.

Concerns were further echoed by respondents to the 2021 EHR survey. In 2021, 15 respondents reported that problems with the quality of data within electronic clinical record system created a barrier to developing national health datasets from this data source. The most commonly expressed concern was with unstructured (free text) data within EHRs that need to be structured following common terminology standards to be readily useable for statistics and research. Thirteen respondents also reported legal restrictions or policy barriers to public authorities extracting data from within EHRs to develop national health datasets.

Perhaps the most difficult barrier is in Switzerland, where the law which authorises the creation of electronic clinical records did not foresee the use of data from within this information system for national statistics or research and, as a result there is a total ban on utilising this information resource for any purpose within the public interest other than directly caring for an individual patient. Similarly, in Korea, the law authorising the Information Exchange Program only authorised the exchange of EHR records for direct patient care and there is no legal basis for the secondary use of EHR data.

In Sweden, whether or not data can be extracted from EHRs for a statistical purpose is limited to whether the specific use has been legally authorised. Statistics and research uses that haven't been already foreseen and legally authorised are restricted. Similarly, Finland's law authorising the EHR system did not specify that health care quality monitoring could be undertaken with data from within the EHR system and are facing restrictions to this activity which is within the public interest. In Iceland, health data registries (datasets) are each authorised by a separate legislation. If a new registry (dataset) is needed, then it is necessary to pass a new legislation to authorise it. Similarly, Portugal reports a lack of legal authorisation to extract data for statistical purposes.

Japan and Turkey report concerns that the national data privacy law restricts their ability to extract data from within their EHR systems to build national datasets that are within the public interest. Canada reports the challenge of having different data protection laws within its 13 provinces and territories.

EU Members are also reporting challenges implementing the *EU General Data Protection Regulation (GDPR)*. Italy reports that the GDPR provisions are complex and required the involvement of the data protection authority to develop effective solutions that support extraction of data from EHRs for statistical purposes. Similarly, Slovenia reports that the national legislation is very sophisticated and restrictive which limits their ability to extract data for statistical purposes.

Principle 4: Clear provision of information to individuals

Clear and understandable information about the processing of personal data should be provided to individuals from whom data has been collected directly. This should include the underlying objectives of the processing, possible lawful access by third parties, the benefits of the processing, and its legal basis. Adherents are also asked to notify individuals in a timely manner of any significant personal data breach. Based on a 2019 survey of Privacy Enforcement Authorities, a recent OECD report captures the trend in OECD countries to pass laws and new expanded mandatory requirements for personal data breach notification (PDBN). Results of the 2019 survey indicate that all respondents bound by the GDPR and more than half of respondents not bound by the GDPR have introduced mandatory PDBN reporting to one or more authorities. More specifically, in the United States, two-thirds of States answered that they had introduced mandatory PDBN reporting to one or more authorities.

The results also indicate that all respondents bound by the GDPR, five of the six respondents not bound by the GDPR, and the US states with mandatory requirements have also put in place mandatory notification of affected data subjects.

Figure 4.2. Number of respondents with mandatory PDBN reporting to one or more authorities

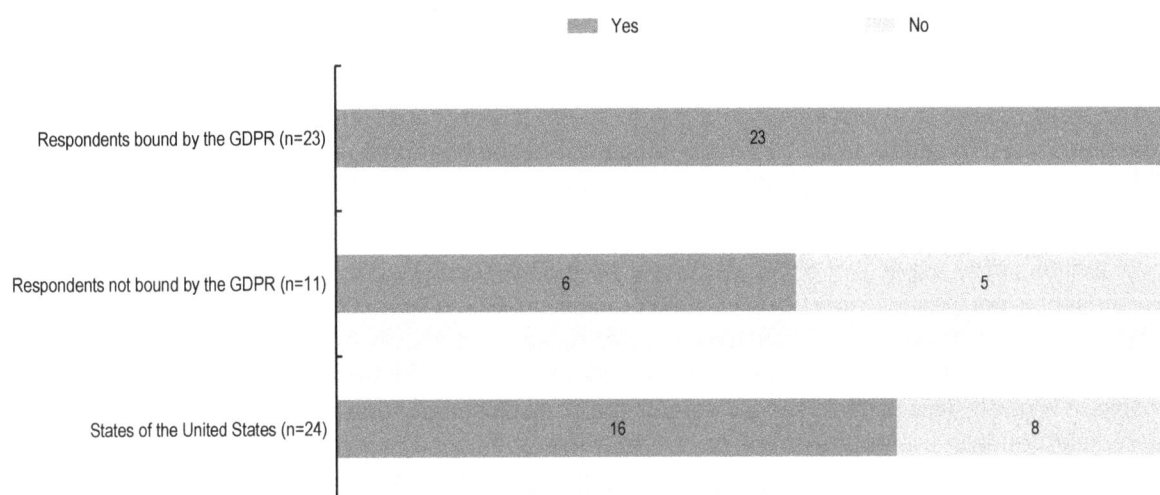

Note: (i) 'Respondents bound by the GDPR'' includes the United Kingdom; (ii) 'Respondents not bound by the GDPR' excludes the United States, and (iii) 'States of the United States': includes responses from 23 States and one US Territory.
Source: Iwaya, Koksal-Oudot and Ronchi (2021[22]), "Promoting Comparability in Personal Data Breach Notification Reporting", https://dx.doi.org/10.1787/88f79eb0-en.

The OECD report identifies the categories of data that Privacy Enforcement Authorities collect through PDBN reporting. The data collected include not only the number of reported PDBNs, but also the nature of the breach (e.g. digital vs non-digital, malicious vs non-malicious, internal vs external), the specific causes (e.g. mailing, hacking, theft), and the types of data breached.

Although health data breaches appear to be on the rise, only 2 respondents reported in 2019-20 that they had experienced a breach of a key national health dataset. No further details about the breaches were provided.

A US law firm providing global services compiles data annually on data security among the clients that it represents that sheds light on digital security threats (BakerHostetler, 2019[23]). The firm reported involvement with over 750 data breaches in 2018, 25% of which were within health care organisations including the pharmaceutical and biotechnology companies. The most common reasons for a data breach were a phishing attack (37%) and a network security hack (30%). The phishing attacks most often involved an email or message that tricked individuals into providing login information that was then used to access the data. Network intrusions occurred most often when servers were internet accessible and unsecured and when devices with file transfer protocols or remote desktops were unsecured. Other reasons for data breaches included inadvertent disclosure (12%), lost or stolen records and devices (10%) and system misconfiguration (4%).

The incidence of data breaches has also been rising. In the United States, the incidence of large data breaches has doubled since 2014. Particularly sharp increases were reported in recent years including a 25% increase from 2019 to 2020 (Alder, 2021[24]). Sixty-seven percent of the breaches in 2020 were related to hacking and exploitation of vulnerabilities in IT systems.

Provision of clear information regarding data processing is discussed in the upcoming section on Principle 7 which focusses on transparency.

Principle 5: Informed consent and appropriate alternatives

Consent mechanisms should provide clarity on whether individual consent is required and the criterion to make this determination; what constitutes valid consent and how it can be withdrawn; and lawful alternatives and exemptions to requiring consent. When data processing is based on consent, the consent should be informed and freely given and individuals provided with mechanisms to provide or withdraw consent to future use of the data. When data processing is not based on consent, individuals should be able to express preferences, including the ability to object to the processing and to actively request that their data be shared. Where data processing requests cannot be honoured, individuals should be provided with the reasons why and the legal basis for the processing.

The discussion of consent during the January 2021 OECD-Israel international workshop was among the most contentious of all aspects of governance that were discussed (Magazanik, 2022[9]). As the principle states, consent is not the only legal basis for data processing. Some workshop participants expressed that if we rely on consent provided during clinical care or research, it should be broad (albeit not a "blanket consent"). That is, consent for future research projects where the concrete aims are not knowable at the time consent is given. This is because re-consenting data subjects for new research uses is impracticable in the context of health system data that cover the whole population; nor for research datasets that are older. Re-consent efforts are not only very expensive, but they also yield data that are biased toward those who are more agreeable to respond, have not moved and are still living. At a health system level there is a need for complete and unbiased data for monitoring and decision-making; and within medical research and machine learning and artificial intelligence algorithm development; biased data result in errors that put patient safety and treatment equity at risk (Oliveira Hashiguchi, Slawomirski and Oderkirk, 2021[16]).

Another challenge is that relying on consent often means relying on the choices of individuals who do not have the time, or the ability, to give full informed consent. Most workshop participants favoured practical opportunities to give consent, while acknowledging the use of other legal basis, when there are benefits in using data, rather than artificially inferring consent. Further, some participants warned that reliance on consent can be accompanied by less attention to privacy-by-design and safeguards protecting data privacy and security, increasing the risk of data breaches. Workshop participants agreed that we ought to ensure that individuals are well informed about the purpose of use of their data, to avoid consequential harm and, most also agreed that we need to seek legislative solutions, rather than always rely on consent as the legal basis for health data collection and processing.

Shortly after this workshop took place, the EDPB (European Data Protection Board) clarified that there is a distinction between the bioethical requirement of informed consent to participate in medical research projects, and Articles 6 and 9 of the GDPR which specify consent as a legal basis for processing personal data and recognise legal basis other than consent, as well as exemptions to explicit consent, as alternative legal grounds to be relied upon for the processing of health data for scientific research purposes or for public interest purposes when it is authorised by member state law. The EDPB distinguishes between interventional research involving the human person and body, where the legal basis is consent, and data and research that is non-interventional in nature where other lawful alternatives to consent may authorise the processing (Magazanik, 2022[9]).

In most respondents all, or nearly all, of the ten key national personal health care datasets included in this study are authorised by law. Thirteen respondents reported that 100% of their key national personal health care datasets were authorised by law and another four respondents reported that 85% or more of these datasets were legally authorised. Patient consent is rarely the legal authorisation for national personal dataset creation in health care.

In three respondents, Norway, Korea and Australia, the national diabetes registry is authorised by patient consent. National emergency care data are authorised by consent in Germany and the United States; prescriptions medicines data are authorised by consent in the United States; and long-term care data are authorised by consent in Australia and the United States. In the Netherlands, prescription medicines and cardiovascular disease registry data are authorised by consent and legislation. In the United States, primary care data are authorised by consent. In Korea, it is possible for next of kin to consent to inclusion of a record in the mortality database.

In more respondents, patients can opt-out of having their information included in a national health care dataset. Patients can opt-out of the majority of national health care datasets in three respondents (France, the Netherlands, and Singapore) and in some states of the United States. In France, the opt-out does not apply to data processing by public bodies. In the Netherlands, opt-out only applies to research uses of in-patient hospitalisation data and for mental hospital in-patient data, opt-out is offered for diagnosis. In the United States, the HIPPA law provides for an opt-out, however, most patients sign a HIPPA disclosure form which allows data sharing for research purposes. Other respondents offering opt-out of health care datasets include Australia (diabetes registry), Belgium (cancer and diabetes registries), Germany (emergency care), and Norway (diabetes and cardiovascular disease registries). In Norway, patients can also opt-out of research uses of cancer registry and formal long-term care data. In Sweden, patients can opt-out of quality registries for CVD conditions, but not from the national dataset. In Korea, it is possible for next of kin to opt-out of inclusion of a record in the mortality database.

In seven respondents, all or nearly all datasets are authorised by a privacy regulatory body or a research ethics committee often in addition to legislative authorisation (Australia, Belgium, Denmark, France, Korea, the Netherlands and the United States). In three respondents, a privacy regulatory body or research ethics committee authorised one national health care dataset: the diabetes registry in Norway, the prescription medicines dataset in Canada, and the cancer registry in Luxembourg.

In Australia and Canada, the authority for the creation of some datasets is a contractual or agreed relationship between national authorities and data suppliers. In Australia, data for hospital and mental hospital in-patients and emergency care are provided for the national datasets under the National Health Information Agreement with data suppliers. The diabetes registry in Australia is developed under a contract between the Department of Health and Diabetes Australia. In Canada, the Canadian Institute for Health Information is a secondary collector of health data, specifically for the planning and management of the health system, including statistical analysis and reporting. Data providers are responsible for meeting the legislative requirements in their respective jurisdictions, where applicable, at the time the data are collected.

In Australia, for the formal long-term care dataset, there is a legal authorisation for data suppliers to provide data to the Australian Institute of Health and Welfare. In the United States, US state laws and regulations authorise the collection of mortality data that is then provided to the federal government for national statistics.

Authority for sharing data within government and with external researchers

The 2019/20 survey asked under what authority national personal health care data could be shared with other government entities or external researchers. Respondents reported that in Denmark, Finland, Germany, Korea, Norway and Slovenia, the sharing of health care datasets is authorised by law for all key health care datasets. In the Austria, Australia, Canada, France, Japan, Luxembourg, the Netherlands and the United States, legislation authorises the data sharing for most key health care datasets that are shared. Legislation authorises the sharing of a minority of datasets in (Belgium, Estonia, Latvia, Singapore and the United Kingdom (Scotland)). In Israel, legislation allows the Central Bureau of Statistics to receive datasets from the health ministry. No sharing of the key health care datasets with other government entities or external researchers is authorised by legislation in Sweden, Ireland, and the Czech Republic.

Far less common is authorising the sharing of health care datasets within government or with external researchers by patient consent. Only in Latvia (eight datasets), United States (five datasets) and Canada (five datasets) did respondents report that patient consent is an authorisation for the sharing of a majority of health care datasets. Three key health care datasets in the Netherlands, two in Korea and Estonia, and one in Australia, Austria, Germany, Norway and the United Kingdom (Scotland) were authorised to be shared by patient consent.

Data subjects were rarely given an opportunity to opt-out of the sharing of key health care datasets. Only respondents in France, the Netherlands and the United States (for some states) reported that one-half or more of key health care datasets had an opt-out of data sharing with government entities or external researchers. Opt-out to data sharing with government entities or external researchers was reported for the sharing of diabetes registry and/or cancer registry data in Sweden, Norway, Luxembourg and Australia. Norway also offers an opt-out to the sharing of long-term care data.

A data privacy protection authority or a research ethics committee authorises the sharing of data with government entities or external researchers for all health care datasets in nine respondents and for the majority of health care datasets in seven respondents. In the United Kingdom (Scotland), Luxembourg and Austria, this was reported as a requirement for sharing one health care dataset. This type of approval was not reported for sharing health care datasets in the Czech Republic, Denmark, Germany and Ireland.

Authorisation of collection and use of Electronic Health Records

Nineteen of 27 respondents to the 2021 EHR survey reported that legislation authorises the collection and use of data within Electronic Health Record (EHR) systems. Twenty-two respondents reported that legislation authorises data extraction from EHR records to create a dataset for government statistics and monitoring. Eighteen respondents reported that legislation authorises the exchange of a patient's EHR data among health care providers who are treating the patient and that legislation authorises the extraction of data from EHR records for approved medical and scientific research projects.

Twelve respondents reported that patient consent is the legal basis for the extraction of data from EHRs for medical or scientific research; 12 reported the same for authorising the exchange of data among health care providers treating a patient; 7 reported the same for the creation of an EHR record; and 4 for the extraction of data for government statistics or monitoring. In most cases, the consent requirement is a complement to legal authorisation of the processing. In Costa Rica, Denmark, Germany, Hungary, Japan, Turkey and the United States; however, consent is sometimes the only authority for EHR collection and/or certain uses.

Some respondents accompany a legal authorisation of processing EHRs with an opportunity for patients to opt-out of the processing of their data. Fifteen respondents reported patients could opt-out of the exchange of data within their own record with other health care providers who are treating them; 10 respondents reported patients could opt-out of the extraction of data from EHRs for approved medical and scientific research, 7 reported the same for the creation of an EHR record and 4 reported the same for the extraction of data for government statistics and monitoring.

Seventeen respondents reported that patient consent or opt-out is collected by health care providers and recorded within the patient's EHR. One respondent indicated that an opt-out is recorded in the EHR by the operator of the EHR system. Fifteen respondents reported that patient consent or opt-out is recorded by patients themselves within a secure Internet patient portal. A minority of respondents (9) reported that consent is collected by health care providers on paper when an EHR is first created. One respondent reported that there is a public website where individuals can look up their health care provider and give consent.

The development of Internet patient portals, where individuals can access their own medical records and can interact with health care providers offers a promising vehicle for managing patient consent and/or opt-out and offers the possibility to make them dynamic such that patients can change their consent or opt-out over time. Turkey offers an interesting approach. Through the utilisation of the e-pulse application and portal, patients can opt out. If they choose so, an SMS will be sent to their mobile phones when a health provider wants to access their data.

Principle 6: Review and approval procedures

Fair and transparent project review processes are important to meeting public expectations regarding appropriate uses of their personal health data. Review and approval procedures should involve an assessment of whether the processing is within the public interest; be robust, objective and fair; be timely; promote consistency in outcomes; be transparent while protecting legitimate interests; and be supported by an independent multi-disciplinary review.

Seventeen respondents reported in 2019/20 that a central authority for the approval of requests to process personal health data is established or planned.

Australia's data governance framework for the My Health Record system, as well as the legislation authorising the system, provide for a central Data Governance Board to manage requests for data from the My Health Record system. The Governance Board is not involved in requests for other national health data; and most of these requests are approved by the Australian Institute of Health and Welfare.

Finland is currently establishing a Health and Social Data Permit Authority (Findata) to approve data processing requests. Denmark has established the Danish Health Data Authority.

In Korea, the Health care Big Data Policy Deliberation Committee supervises and manages the Korea Health Industry Development Institute, which is responsible for information strategy planning, and the National Evidence-based Health care Collaboration Agency, which is responsible for undertaking dataset linkages.

In Belgium, the Information Security Committee is responsible for approving requests to process personal health data; in Luxembourg, the National Commission for Data Protection grants approvals; and in France the data protection authority (CNIL) approves the creation of datasets and the processing of data. Similarly, in Estonia, the Data Protection Inspectorate approves requests to process personal health data. There are research ethics committees in Estonia that are also involved in project approvals. In Israel, the Ministry of Health's Data Delivery Committee approves requests in co-ordination with the Privacy Protection Authority of the Ministry of Justice.

In The Netherlands, organisations can create datasets and can undertake dataset linkages under the precondition that their activities meet the requirements of the GDPR and the *Medical Treatment Act*. The Data Protection Authority evaluates whether datasets meet GDPR requirements. Further guidelines regarding necessary elements of quality registries are also provided by the national body overseeing the electronic health record system (NICTIZ).

In Slovenia, new datasets must be authorised by law and all other cases of data processing are approved by the Information Commissioner. Likewise, the Swedish Ethical Review Authority approves requests for data processing for research projects; however, multi-purpose datasets require legal authorisation before they can be created. In Sweden, data custodians also independently approve data requests.

In Norway, there are regional research ethics committees and a national centre for research data (REK) that assesses requests for health data processing in terms of research methods, an assessment of benefits/risks and data privacy safeguards.

In Canada, provinces and territories have individual processes for approval of requests to process personal health data. To support knowledge creation and help researchers, policy makers and decision-makers make more effective use of pan-Canadian data, the Heath Data Research Network's Data Access Support Hub (DASH) allows Canadian researchers requiring multi-jurisdictional data to request data from a single source.

In Germany, there are plans to open national electronic health record data for research, but it is not yet clear whether a single authority for data access management would be created or whether the organisation that is currently responsible for e-HR infrastructure would assume this task.

Current regulations in Ireland provide for a Consent Declaration Committee to adjudicate health research requests involving consent exemptions. As Ireland develops an information strategy, a national health information office may be set up that would provide the necessary approvals for persons or organisations seeking dataset linkages and access to linked data for valid purposes.

In Latvia, the Centre for Disease Prevention and Control evaluates researchers' and research institutions' applications for the use of identifiable patient data recorded in the medical documents in specific research under Cabinet Regulation No. 446 which covers cases where it is not possible to obtain informed consent from the patient. If approved, data for research from different sources is provided/available on a person level with a direct identifier (personal ID, etc.). Requests for a data extraction from the public monitoring system for health care quality and efficiency are approved by a special project council consisting of representatives from the Centre for Disease Prevention and Control, National Health Service, State Emergency Medical Service and Health Inspectorate. In this case, approved applicants access pseudonymised data.

Information Services Scotland (ISS) sets out criteria for approval to access data within a safe haven environment. Applicants must be employed by an approved organisation and meet other requirements, such as undertaking training in information governance requirements. Applicants seeking a dataset linkage may be required to apply for approval by the NHS Scotland Public Benefit and Privacy Panel.

In the United States, most health care providers must follow the HIPAA Privacy Rule which sets a baseline protection for certain individually identifiable health information. The Rule permits, but does not require, covered health care providers to give patients a choice regarding whether their health information is disclosed or exchanged electronically with others for key purposes including treatment, payment and health care operations. The Privacy Rule also sets standards for the sharing of protected health information for research purposes and for creating and disclosing de-identified and limited data sets.

Principle 7: Transparency through public information

The Recommendation recommends that Adherents establish and implement national health data governance frameworks that provide for transparency through public information mechanisms that do not compromise health data privacy or security protections or organisations' commercial or other legitimate interests. Public information should include the purpose of the processing, the health-related public interest served, the legal basis for the processing, the procedure and criteria used to approve the processing, a summary of approval decisions taken, and information about the implementation of the national framework and how effective it has been.

Clarity and transparency supports protecting individual's privacy and autonomy while also ensuring that data processors and data users are aware of the authority under which data may be used and can plan the development of research programmes accordingly.

Twenty-one respondents reported in 2019-20 that for all or most key health care datasets there is a publicly available description of the dataset purpose and content and most provided a web-link to this public information. Singapore reported that a public description was available for two datasets; and Ireland reported this for one dataset.

Seventeen respondents reported that the description of all or most health care datasets includes the health-related public interests served by the data. Seventeen respondents reported that the description for all or most datasets includes the legal basis for the processing: Austria, Belgium, Canada, the Czech Republic, Denmark, Finland, France, Germany, Israel, Korea, Latvia, Luxembourg, the Netherlands, Norway, Slovenia, Sweden and the United Kingdom (Scotland).

The procedure to request access to the data and the criteria used to approve access to the data are publicly available for all or most health care datasets in 17 respondents: Australia, Belgium, Canada, the Czech Republic, Denmark, France, Germany, Israel, Japan, Korea, Latvia, the Netherlands, Norway, Slovenia, Sweden, United Kingdom (Scotland) and the United States.

Fourteen respondents reported that the procedure to request a record linkage or other further processing of all or most health care datasets and the criteria used to approve these requests are publicly available: Australia, Belgium, Canada, Denmark, Finland, France, Israel, Japan, Korea, Latvia, the Netherlands, Sweden and the United Kingdom (Scotland).

When asked if there is a summary of approval decisions for the record linkage or further processing of the datasets that is publicly available, 10 respondents answered yes for all or most key health care datasets: Australia, Denmark, Finland, France, Israel, Japan, Korea, Latvia, Sweden, and the United Kingdom (Scotland). When asked whether the summary describes or identifies the data recipient of an approved record linkage or further processing of the datasets, only Denmark, France, Israel, Japan, Korea, Latvia, Sweden, and the United Kingdom (Scotland) said yes for all or most health care datasets.

Principle 8: Development of technology

The Recommendation recommends that Adherents establish and implement national health data governance frameworks that maximise the potential and promote the development of technology as a means of enabling the re-use and analysis of health data while protecting privacy and security and facilitating individual's control of uses of their own data.

The January 2021 OECD-Israel international workshop explored state-of-the-art technologies that support access to health data while protecting privacy (Magazanik, 2022[9]). Emerging concepts and mechanisms include de-identification, differential privacy, homomorphic encryption, synthetic data, multi-party computation, distributed analytics and real-time remote data access. Each of these mechanisms, however, is context-dependent and presents unique benefits and limitations.

New technologies for data governance

Privacy-by-design best practices involve a combination of privacy enhancing technologies with data access processes and tools. Privacy-by-design encourages consideration of data protection at all stages of data development, use, sharing and access; and in the design of IT systems for data management. These principles serve as a risk mitigation tool. An example of a privacy-by-design practice raised during the workshop is the use of 'containers' for storing data both on an organisation's premises and on the cloud service because data are encrypted when they move between containers.

Participants discussed that while de-identification is essential, de-identification techniques can still leave microdata vulnerable to a risk of unapproved or malicious re-identification attack. Efforts to achieve anonymity through de-identification can render data unlinkable for future research and statistics and data can be so heavily perturbed as to become not granular enough or accurate enough for medical research. Pseudonymised data, where the keys to re-identify the data are securely and separately stored, can support future approved research involving dataset linkages. In general, de-identified microdata require additional safeguards when they are shared or linked.

Synthetic data are not real and thus data protection and privacy law does not apply to them. A workshop participant shared experience with a solution that generates synthetic data from real data while maintaining data integrity. The system generates a report describing how closely the synthetic data match the real data. Clinicians are using the system to create their own synthetic datasets without needing programmers to prepare the dataset for them. A caveat with synthetic data is that they are usually accurate enough for preparing final research results, for machine learning or for training AI algorithms; and therefore ethical approval to access/run programmes on the original data would still be needed.

There were discussions of three different solutions to the challenge of undertaking multi-site studies, particularly where they involve data from multiple countries. In the first solution, which was applied by the SCOR consortium for COVID-19 research, homomorphic encryption of personal health datasets was applied to allow the datasets to be safely shared with other researchers who can apply computations to the data and receive results but cannot see or decrypt the dataset. A caveat of this technique is that researchers cannot identify or correct for errors in the underlying data and they can use only a limited set of analytical techniques.

A second methodology of the SCOR consortium is secure multi-party computation where each researcher in a consortium can run computations on their own personal health dataset without disclosing more about their data to the consortium partners than what they can learn from the research outputs. A limitation of this method is that it may require all researchers to be on-line when the computation is run. The SCOR consortium is working to reduce the constraints of each of these methods by combining homomorphic encryption and multi-party computation to enables all consortium members to run computations on all of the partners data as if all of the data were stored in a single location (Raisaro, 2020[25]).

A challenge raised at the workshop is that encryption is not seen as anonymisation for the purposes of adherence to privacy regulations and it is not clear yet how the EU GDPR may apply to the method used by SCOR consortium partners within Europe.

Another potential solution was a federated data model. The EHDEN project fosters trust with a distributed analytics framework, where software and statistical analysis programmes travel to where data are located, rather than data flowing to a central data lake for analysis (EHDEN, 2021[26]). With this method, data collectors retain control of their data at all times and data privacy and security remain protected by local legal requirements and operational practices. Data collectors also pseudonymise their own data before they are analysed. Further, because there is no transfer of record-level data, associated security risks are avoided. Key to the success of this method is the coding of data within the Federation to a common data model (OMOP) which permits the analytical programmes or software code to run smoothly at each node of the network. EHDEN is coding more than 327 million pseudonymised health records from 60 partners in 20 countries to the OMOP common data model.

Some participants at the workshop argued that the future is, or should be, based on a federated model of citizens holding their own data. On the other hand, others raised the concern that not all useful analytical techniques should be applied to data within a federated model. For example, the Cox proportional hazards regression model that is used for survival analysis (for example, cancer survival estimates) fails to yield an unbiased result when applied to data in a federated structure. Work on methods to overcome this limitation, however, are developing (Andreux, 2020[27]).

New analytical technologies

A small number of respondents are utilising new technologies to increase the analytical value and information and tool development potential of their electronic health record systems. In 2021, eight respondents reported applying data mining to find or extract data within their EHR systems. Eight respondents reported applying machine learning/artificial intelligence algorithms to EHR systems data for alerts or messages regarding patient care or managerial decision-making and seven reported utilising predictive analytics for the same reasons. Six respondents reported national projects to integrate or link EHR data with genomic, environmental, behavioural, economic or other data. Respondents reporting three or four of these new technologies were Costa Rica, Denmark, Israel, and the Netherlands and respondents reporting two of these technologies were Estonia, Finland, Luxembourg, Portugal and Sweden.

Respondents also invested in new technologies to manage the COVID-19 pandemic. In 2021, respondents to the EHR survey were asked about making a connection or integrating EHR systems to track and trace patients infected with SarsCoV2; to issue COVID-19 vaccination certificates; and to conduct post-market surveillance of the safety and effectiveness of the COVID-19 vaccines. Nineteen respondents reported utilising at least one of these three technologies and seven respondents reported all three (Turkey, Slovenia, the Netherlands, Lithuania, Israel, Iceland, and Denmark). Blockchain technology also has emerging and potential uses in health care as well as data protection challenges (OECD, 2020[17]).

Further discussion on the development of new privacy enhancing technologies is presented in the section on Principle 11 – Controls and Safeguards, particularly the development of new distributed analytics techniques in the United Kingdom (OpenSAFELY) and Korea (OHDISI) to increase research access to timely data to respond to the COVID-19 pandemic.

Principle 9: Monitoring and evaluation

Monitoring and evaluation mechanisms should assess whether the uses of personal health data have met the intended public interest purposes and brought the benefits expected. This should include reporting on negative consequences including failures to comply with data protection and privacy laws and data security requirements and data breaches and misuses.

Assessment results should be used for continuous improvement including periodic reviews of developments in personal health data availability, the needs of health research and public policy needs and reviews of policies and practices to protect privacy and data security. Adherents should also encourage those processing health data to review the capabilities and vulnerabilities of the technologies they use.

The OECD assists Members and Non-Members in monitoring their progress through our regular programme of surveys of health data development, use and governance that are undertaken by the Health Care Quality and Outcomes Working Party on 5-year cycle. Beginning in 2021, the OECD further assists countries, on their request, with a detailed review of health information systems where the analytical framework is the Council Recommendation on Health Data Governance.

For individual countries, reforms to health data development, use and governance are still evolving, particularly due to changes brought about to manage the COVID-19 pandemic. Further measurement of Adherents engagement in self-monitoring and evaluation would be more appropriate during the next monitoring period of the Recommendation (2022-27).

Principle 10: Training and skill development

The Recommendation recommends that Adherents establish and implement national health data governance frameworks that establish training and skill development in privacy and data security measures for those processing personal health data that are in line with prevailing standards and data processing techniques.

The 2019/20 survey asked respondents if the organisations responsible for 10 key national health care datasets provide regular training to staff regarding their responsibilities to protect privacy and data security.

Sixteen respondents reported that regular training was provided to staff across all of the organisations responsible for all key health care datasets. The United Kingdom (Scotland) reported that this was the case for the majority of key health care datasets. Six respondents did not confirm that regular staff training is provided for most key national health care datasets (Norway, Japan, Israel, Ireland, Germany, and Estonia).

In Belgium, Canada, the Czech Republic, Korea, and Latvia training is provided when staff start a new job and then annually afterward. Training is provided annually in Denmark and the United States. United Kingdom (Scotland) provides training when staff start a new job and then every 2 years afterwards. Slovenia provides training when staff start a new job and then every 3-4 years afterward. In Luxembourg, training is provided when staff start a new job and then on an ad hoc basis afterward. Singapore provides training when staff start a new job or gain access to a new dataset. Sweden provides training when staff start a new job involving the health registries. In Australia, training in data privacy and security protection is provided for new staff or when there are changes in legislation and at other regular intervals. Similarly, training is provided in Finland at the start of employment and when necessary afterward, such as when there are changes in legislation.

Training is provided to new staff and to all staff annually for some health care datasets in Estonia (cancer registry, cardiovascular disease registry and mortality data) and for the cancer registry in Japan. Training is provided in Germany for staff processing hospital in-patient data at 1-2 year intervals.

In Austria and the Netherlands, the frequency of staff training depends on each organisation's internal rules and practices. Most organisations in the Netherlands, however, reported training staff who were starting a new job.

Principle 11: Controls and Safeguards

National health data governance frameworks should provide for implementation of controls and safeguards. Principle 11 sets out the following specific controls and safeguards that should be in place when processing personal health data.

- Controls and safeguards when processing personal health data should include clear lines of accountability, mechanisms for audit, formal risk management processes including risks of unwanted data erasure, re-identification, breaches or other misuses.

- Processing should be limited to organisations with appropriate data privacy and security training for staff members who process data. Organisations processing health data should designate an employee(s) to be responsible for the information security programme, including informing staff of their legal obligations.

- Technological, physical and organisational measures should include: mechanisms that limit the identification of individuals through de-identification of personal health data, and take into account the proposed use of the data and allow for data re-identification for approved future data analysis or to inform an individual of a research outcome.

- Agreements when sharing data with third parties should specify arrangements for the secure transfer of data and include means to sanction non-compliance. Where practicable, alternatives to transferring data should be considered such as secure data access centres and remote data access facilities.
- Measures should also include robust identity verification and authentication of individuals processing personal health data.

This section presents results of the 2021 OECD survey that asked about the secure exchange of electronic clinical records and the 2019-20 OECD survey that asked a series of specific questions to processors of respondents' 12 key national health datasets including:

- Designated official responsible for data protection,
- Controlling access to personal health data,
- Data de-identification,
- Risk management,
- Data sharing agreements,
- Data transfers to approved applicants, and
- Alternatives to data transfers: Research Data Centres and Remote Data Access.

Designated official responsible for data protection

Organisations often designate an employee or employees to co-ordinate and be accountable for the organisation's information security programme, including informing the organisation and its employees of their legal responsibilities to protect privacy and data security.

Most respondents have a data protection or privacy official within the data custodian's offices for all of their national health care datasets. In respondents within the European Economic Area, the requirements of data protection officers within data processors are set out in the *EU General Data Protection Regulation*.

In Germany and the United Kingdom (Scotland) there was an officer reported for the majority of national health care datasets. In Norway, a national data protection or privacy official was not reported within the organisations responsible for health care datasets. In Ireland, the only custodian of a national health care dataset reported to have a data protection officer was the custodian of the national hospital in-patient dataset.

The main responsibilities of the data protection/privacy officer within organisations processing health care data are similar across respondents. Principally, these officers ensure that all aspects of the processing of personal health data are done in conformity with legal requirements for data protection, which often involves developing internal policies and guidelines, and providing education and advisory services to staff. In some respondents, they may have additional responsibilities, such as the ethical use of data in Singapore and the United States; data de-identification/pseudonymisation and disclosure mitigation in Belgium, Israel, the Czech Republic and the United States; and for cyber security in the Czech Republic.

Controlling access to personal health data

Identities of staff accessing all key national health care datasets are controlled and tracked in 14 respondents and for most national health care datasets in 4 respondents. In Sweden, employees are authorised to access datasets, as required, and usage is not tracked; with the exception of the cancer registry where usage is logged. The control and tracking of the identities of staff accessing the majority of national personal health care datasets in Germany, Ireland, Israel, and Norway was not reported.

Slovenia uses personal digital certificates to track the identities of individuals accessing personal health data. Luxembourg restricts access to authorised persons and every dataset access is logged. In Latvia, authorisation is only possible with internet bank access details, electronic ID or electronic signature (for E-health system) or username and password (for other health data systems). Further, all access to personal health data is audited. In Finland, staff must have permission to access data, the access is password protected and usage is logged.

Staff approved to access SNDS data in France, access the data via a secure portal that authenticates users and tracks usage. In the United States, staff must complete a data user access request form detailing the folders and files they will be accessing. Access to data is provided through a Research Data Centre.

In Korea, only authorised personnel are allowed access and the data cannot be stored on a storage device, such as USB. Estonia also restricts access to authorised personnel and, for some datasets, logs activity. In Canada, some datasets require a user-id and a password to access while other datasets maintain access and activity logs. Australia and the Czech Republic restrict access to authorised personnel. In Belgium there is a data access management process.

Denmark is revising its practices in response to changes to regulations and to a re-organisation of health data processors.

Data de-identification

Seventeen respondents reported in 2019-20 that all of their key health care datasets are de-identified prior to analysis. This is also the case for the majority of health care datasets in four respondents. Norway and Ireland did not report that data are de-identified prior to analysis.

Fifteen respondents reported that pseudonyms are created for direct identifiers on all of their health care datasets and four respondents reported this was the case for most of their health care datasets. Reversible pseudonyms facilitate re-identification to conduct future approved data linkages and analysis or to inform an individual of a specific condition or research outcome, where appropriate.

Risk Management

Thirteen respondents reported in 2019-20 that there is a process for the assessment of the risk of data re-identification for all or the majority of their health care datasets. In contrast, in 10 countries, assessment of data re-identification risk is not done or is done for only one or two health care datasets.

Nine respondents reported that there are practices for the treatment of variables that pose a re-identification risk (such as rare diseases, exact dates, locations, or ethnic origins) for all of their key health care datasets. Another 10 respondents reported that this was the case for most of their key health care datasets. Four respondents did not report these practices (Austria, Ireland, Norway and Slovenia).

The United Kingdom (Scotland) reported techniques to protect against data re-identification including table redesign, supressing values and swapping records. Singapore reported using data suppression, grouping values and randomising shifts in values. Canada reported using data suppression, truncation of values and grouping, and for mortality data rounding to a base of 5. Japan and Australia reported grouping values and supressing values. The Czech Republic, Israel, Luxembourg and Latvia reported grouping values. Estonia reported supressing values, including where variables represent less than five cases. Denmark reported rounding values and supressing variables representing less than five cases. Belgium and the United States reported grouping, suppression and data masking, as well as restricting some data in Belgium to aggregated data only and, in the United States, creating restricted data files. Korea reported grouping values and supressing values. Most data custodians in the Netherlands reported grouping values and some reporting supressing values. Germany reported not using exact dates within cancer registry data and Japan reported grouping and supressing values in the cancer registry.

Few respondents reported conducting testing on all or the majority of datasets to ensure that realistic re-identification attacks will have a very small probability of success: Denmark, France, Korea, Singapore,

HEALTH DATA GOVERNANCE FOR THE DIGITAL AGE © OECD 2022

United Kingdom (Scotland) and the United States (Annex B.40). Belgium, Germany, Luxembourg, the Netherlands and Sweden reported conducting this testing on some of their health care datasets.

In Sweden, the main effort is prevention of data intruders. All data at the National Board of Health and Welfare are managed and placed in a separate network/servers. The lock to access the network is supervised and logged. This is handled in a similar way at the diabetes register. A few years ago, ethical hackers were engaged to test the strength of the protection against intrusion. France reported testing re-identification by using external information. Both France and Sweden indicated that their main effort is directed toward preventing data intruders, such as secure storage and access to data and access controls.

Korea reported using an encryption technique where data are made unintelligible to all except holders of the decryption key and testing the risk of unauthorised decryption. Denmark uses a method similar to that of Korea when data are to be shared with external researchers. Luxembourg reported using data security auditing for the cancer registry. The Netherlands reported using software developed to detect re-identification risk for mortality data. Belgium reported disclosure risk assessment to ensure that released data has 5 or more cases per cell. Singapore reported testing the data anonymisation process. Denmark reported that the testing methods are under development.

Data sharing agreements

Eighteen respondents reported that they have a standard data sharing agreement for disclosing data from all or the majority of their health care datasets (Annex B.49). A standard data sharing agreement was reported for one dataset in Ireland. The use of standard data sharing agreements was not reported in Austria, the Czech Republic, Estonia, and Norway.

Standard data sharing agreements include requirements for certain data privacy and security practices at the data recipient's site for all or the majority of health care datasets shared by 16 respondents(Australia, Belgium, Canada, Denmark, Finland, France, Israel, Japan, Korea, Luxembourg, the Netherlands, Singapore, Slovenia, Sweden, United Kingdom (Scotland) and the United States).

Examples of the requirements for data privacy and security practices in standard data sharing agreements include:

- Qualified personnel,
- Secure data storage,
- Data use is in accordance with applicable laws,
- Data is used only for approved purposes,
- Secure physical site where data is held,
- Data access is restricted via a secure server (remote access),
- Data access is restricted to authorised staff,
- Data destruction date is respected,
- No unauthorised data linkages,
- No unauthorised data sharing,
- No attempt at data re-identification,
- Disclosure rules applied to published statistics and research findings,
- Training in data privacy and security protection, and
- Adherence to national or international standards for IT security.

Seven respondents reported providing training to data recipients regarding data privacy and security practices when all or the majority of health care datasets are shared (Austria, Demark, Finland, France, Korea, United Kingdom (Scotland) and the United States). Estonia provides training when cancer registry and mortality data are shared, the Netherlands provides training when mental hospital in-patient data and mortality data are shared, and Ireland provides training when hospital in-patient data are shared.

The United States offers on-line training. In-person instruction is provided in Estonia. One-on-one meetings or trainings are reported in the Netherlands and Finland. France requires training take place before data access can be approved. United Kingdom (Scotland) trains on the Medical Research Council requirements for research, GDPR requirements and data confidentiality protection.

The survey asked whether data sharing agreements include penalties that would occur if the required data privacy and security practices were not respected. Penalties were reported as included in standard data sharing agreements in Australia, Canada, Estonia, Finland, Germany, Japan, Korea, Latvia, Luxembourg, the Netherlands, Singapore, Sweden, United Kingdom (Scotland) and the United States.

Data transfers to approved applicants

Respondents were asked if they transfer data to approved applicants, such as by sending a copy of a dataset. This method is used for transferring all health care datasets to approved applicants in 11 respondents and for transferring some key health care datasets in another 9 respondents. Fourteen respondents in 2019/20 reported secure portals/file transfer protocols to transfer data over the internet (Australia, Belgium, Canada, Denmark, Finland, Germany, Ireland, Israel, Korea, Luxembourg, the Netherlands, Singapore, United Kingdom (Scotland) and the United States).

A few respondents were encrypting the data and sending it to the recipient on a USB stick or CD: Sweden, Slovenia, Latvia, and Japan, In Estonia, the encrypted data may be sent by e-mail, by using a cloud transfer mechanism and by USB stick. In Canada, data is sometimes encrypted and sent on a CD and in Korea, it is sometimes sent on a USB stick.

Alternatives to transfers – remote data access and research data centres

Alternatives to data transfers to third parties include secure research data access centres and remote data access facilities. In 2019-20, 11 respondents out of 23 provided secure access to all or most de-identified national health datasets via remote data access, a research data centre or both (Austria, Denmark, France, Israel, Korea, Luxembourg, the Netherlands, Singapore, Slovenia, United Kingdom (Scotland) and the United States).

Remote data access is a service providing access to data stored on a computer or network from a remote distance. Remote data access services are often secured to ensure that users can only access data to which they have been approved and that users cannot alter or withdraw/copy the data from the system without permission.

Six respondents provide access to all or most key health care datasets to external approved applicants via a remote data access facility: United Kingdom (Scotland), Luxembourg, Korea, France, Denmark and Austria. Sweden and Belgium offer remote data access to the diabetes registry. Germany and the Netherlands provide remote access to in-patient hospital data. The Netherlands also has this service for access to mental hospital in-patient data, CVD registry and mortality data. Finland has this service for mortality data. Australia offers remote data access to primary care and prescription medicines data via an enterprise data warehouse.

A research data centre is a secure physical setting, such as a secure room, where access is provided to data. Research data centres may have physical security, such as supervision and locked doors, as well as computer and data security, such as computer systems that ensure users can only access data to which they have been approved and that users cannot alter or withdraw/copy data from the system without permission.

A research data centre is provided for all or most health care datasets in seven respondents: Denmark, Israel, Korea, Singapore, Slovenia, United Kingdom (Scotland) and the United States (Annex B.52). Australia offers a research data centre for primary care data, prescription medicines data, and long-term care data; Austria offers this service for hospital in-patient, cancer registry and mortality data; the Netherlands offers this service for CVD registry, long-term care and mortality data; and Canada offers this service for cancer registry and mortality data. A few more respondents offer a research data centre for one dataset: Sweden for diabetes registry data, Germany for hospital inpatient data, Finland for mortality data and Belgium and Luxembourg for cancer registry data.

Australian national authorities use remote access data laboratories for analysing routinely collected data, allowing researchers to log in remotely and securely analyse data. For the diabetes registry in Belgium, remote data access is provided via virtual desktops with SAS Enterprise Guide, connected to a SAS server and a DB2 database. In Luxembourg, a government cloud environment is used to create one virtual office per project where approved applicants access the data by state internal network or VPN with strong user authentication. In Sweden for the diabetes registry data, the remote access service is called SODA – Secure Online Data Access. SODA users cannot download or copy data and can only perform data analysis.

In the Netherlands, hospital in-patient and mental hospital in-patient data are accessible through a remote data access service of Statistics the Netherlands. A remote data access service for long-term care data is provided within the Vektis Institute. Research data centres are provided for CVD registry and mortality data.

In France, the law restricts the processing of data to secure environments that conform with security requirements. Access to national de-identified health care data is via secure remote data access platforms provided by organisations meeting these security requirements. The linked health care administrative data in France (SNDS) are accessible via a platform operated by CNAM. Other platforms also provide remote access to health data, such as a platform for accessing hospital data managed by ATIH, and a platform offering access to a broad range of economic and social data via a Centre for Secure Data Access (CASD) on behalf of several public organisations.

In Austria, the secure research data centre is called SafeCentre and is provided by Statistics Austria. In Korea, the Remote Analysis System is managed by the National Health Insurance Service (NHIS) and the Health Insurance Review and Assessment Service (HIRA).

In the United States, access to de-identified personal health data (restricted data) is provided within research data centres of the National Centre for Health Statistics, which has four locations on the east coast, and also via a network of statistical research data centres managed by the US Census Bureau, which has sites across the country.

In the research data centre for the cancer registry in Belgium, data users access a computer that is part of a system that limits data access to only approved datasets and prevents users from downloading or copying data without permission. In Slovenia, there is a special room within a secured building that is without internet connection and provides users with access to several standard software packages (SPSS, SAS, MS).

Finland has launched a new Health and Social Data Permit Authority (Findata) to promote the secondary use of health and social data, facilitate the process to authorise data access and protect data privacy and security. As part of this effort, Finland is developing a remote data access service that will provide access to the majority of national health datasets.

In Canada, the Canadian Institute for Health Information is developing a secure analytic environment for data access to national health care datasets where researchers and other data users can access data virtually. The secure analytical environment will also allow for more timely access, as well increased security through enhancements to de-identification. Some health datasets are accessible in Canada via Statistics Canada's Research Data Centres which are located across the country.

The number of analysts accessing health care datasets in research data centres or via remote data access services varies a lot by dataset in many respondents. The highest number of annual external data users was reported by Korea and France. Korea reported over 3 000 external analysts accessing the national health care data of NHIS and HIRA (1 500 each) per year. Since 2017, France has received 450 applications for access to the national linked health administrative data (SNDS). Australia reported over 1 000 external analysts accessing long-term care data each year, but relatively fewer accessing hospital in-patient data (100) and emergency care data (50). The United States reported over 1 000 external analysts accessing mortality data. The number of external data users varied by health care dataset from 1 to 500 in the Netherlands; 33 to 300 in Sweden; 10 to100 in Finland; from 5 to 83 per year in Canada; about 40 in Germany; from 4 to 20 in Estonia; under 100 in Singapore; and 2 to 20 in Slovenia.

Access to data for COVID-19 research

In 2020 and 2021 there has been an expansion of efforts to develop secure mechanisms for researchers to access and use health data. The following are examples of activities to increase access to and use of data for research from the OECD 2021 Survey of Developments in Health Data and Governance as a result of the COVID-19 Pandemic ("COVID-19 Survey").

In the United Kingdom, the National Health Service in England partnered with a private company (Palantir) to develop a Foundry platform, which enables bespoke and rapid data dashboard development and a tool to manage data access requests and data flows in a secure way. Before the pandemic hit, NHS England was developing trusted research environments (TREs) which protect – by design – the privacy of individuals whose health data they hold, while facilitating large scale data analysis using high performance computing (NHS Digital, 2021[28]). Approved researchers who sign a data sharing agreement are given access to a secure remote data access environment that hosts analysis and interrogation tools including Databricks (supporting SQL and Python languages) and RStudio (statistical programming language). Researchers with the same data sharing agreement can work collaboratively with their colleagues in shared project folders, using their preferred tool. The final intended output is checked for compliance with data protection requirements before data exports are approved. During the COVD-19 pandemic, the TRE was expanded to include COVID-19 related data including vaccination data contributed from the Office of National Statistics.

The OpenSAFELY project in the United Kingdom (England) accelerates the availability of research using electronic clinical records of general practitioners (OpenSAFELY, 2021[29]). OpenSAFELY is a secure, open-source software platform for analysis of electronic health records data. Approved researchers develop code for statistical analysis using dummy data and open tools and services like GitHub. Their code is automatically tested by OpenSAFELY tools and when it is capable of running to completion, it is sent to a live data environment to be executed against real patient data. Researchers can only view their results tables and graphs and cannot view real patient data or enter the environment where the real data are held. All platform activity is publicly logged. Code for data management and analysis are shared for scientific review and re-use. OpenSAFELY software was deployed within the secure data centres of the two largest electronic health record providers in the NHS.

Prior to the pandemic, Wales in the United Kingdom already benefitted from an internationally renowned platform supporting the record linkage of health data as well as data from other fields (e.g. education and social care). The Secure Anonymised Information Linkage (SAIL) Databank provides robust secure storage of de-identified person-based data for research to improve health, well-being and services. The Welsh Multimorbidity e-Cohort (WMC), was designed to aid analysis on the implications of multiple chronic illnesses by measuring prevalence, trajectories and determinants, as well as helping to identify clusters of diseases that result in the greatest health care need and death. The WMC was repurposed for rapid analysis to support the response to COVID-19 in Wales. As a result of WMC, the new de-identified datasets available through SAIL grew to include Census data from the Office of National Statistics (ONS) and data on school workforce, education attendance, and COVID-19 symptoms, vaccination, shielded people, test results, track and trace and viral sequence. Policy makers benefited from timely analysis of the pandemic and the research community benefited from increased availability of data, subject to SAIL Databank's strict governance and application process.

In the United Kingdom, Public Health Scotland collaborated with Higher Education Institutions to create a comprehensive repository for COVID-19 research in Scotland. This fully searchable COVID-19 Research Repository reduces duplication of effort and makes it easier for policy makers, researchers and the public to find and use research results.

Sweden established a fast-track to accelerate the processing of requests for access to data and statistics for COVID-19 related research from all major data-holders and has also created a fast-track for applications to ethical review-boards for COVID-19 research projects and for permits for clinical trials.

Australia has made improvements to its existing data request system to make it easier to obtain data, including enabling researchers to have access to linked data sets in a "one-stop-shop" arrangement. There is also a mechanism for sharing de-identified data with an Australian research institute to support modelling, and to support further advice to the government. The Australian Government Department of Health is progressing a number of projects that aim to streamline researcher access to de-identified health data within Australia, including upgrades to existing data request forms, risk assessment tools, ICT infrastructure, and protocol arrangements with Australian Government statistical agencies. Together, these upgrades aim to clarify and rationalise data access processes that researchers have to navigate to use Australians' health information for research purposes.

In Spain, anonymised data from the test result system, the vaccination system, the hospital capacity and occupancy system, the SIVIES System, and others have been shared through an automatic process with public universities to provide inputs into forecast models. In Italy, Agenas has implemented the "System for assessing the resilience capacity of the National Health System", in collaboration with the School of Advanced Studies – Pisa, which aims to measure the capacity of the various regional systems to maintain service delivery levels during the COVID-19 pandemic.

In the United States, the Centers for Disease Control and Prevention (CDC)'s data repository (Data.CDC.gov) provides public access to 69 COVID-19 specific datasets, including three COVID-19 case surveillance datasets available for public use. Also developed were COVID-19 Case Surveillance Restricted Access Detailed Data which are de-identified patient-level data including clinical and symptom data, demographics, and state and county of residence. These patient-level data are reported by US states and autonomous reporting entities to the US Centers for Disease Control and Prevention (CDC). Access to the data for research requires a simply but secure registration process and a data use agreement and application information is available on data.cdc.gov. The dataset is stored on a secure GitHub repository.

In Korea, the Health Insurance Review and Assessment Service (HIRA) established and shared COVID-19 personal health datasets for international research collaboration. The health data on infectious disease treatment were stored within the closed network of HIRA and were coded to a global common data model (OMOP). Researchers could access only the data schema (structure and variables) to prepare statistical programmes (coding) or submit queries through a tool (ATLAS). This was a partial application of CDM-based distributed research as part of the OHDISI project, which shares not the data itself but the grounds. The merits of this approach include opening data for a large group of domestic and international researchers for collaborative research while protecting data privacy and security within HIRA. Data accessibility was accelerated by having an IRB exemption and a simplified application process. The National Health Insurance Service (NHIS) links and de-identifies national health insurance claims data to COVID-19 confirmed patient data, vaccination and adverse event data from the Korea Disease Control and Prevention Agency (KDCA), and provides the dataset to external researchers in a closed environment.

Further, the Public Institutional Bioethics Review Board (IRB) of Korea National Institute for Bioethics Policy decided to exempt IRB review for COVID-19 research, so the data utilisation could be more timely.

Secure exchange of electronic clinical records

Surprisingly, given the mounting volume of data, only 8 of 26 respondents in 2021 reported that EHR data are stored or processed using Cloud Computing services (Australia, Israel, Japan, Korea, Luxembourg, the Netherlands, Portugal and the United States). The majority of respondents are still managing EHRs with dedicated governmental servers.

Fourteen respondents reported that clinical data are encrypted when they are exchanged to protect privacy and data security. Nine respondents reported that clinical data are exchanged using a dedicated, secure network. Security measures for these networks included a digital signature for ID (Denmark), digital signature with smartcard (Luxembourg, the Netherlands), multi-factor authentication (Canada, Italy, the Netherlands, Switzerland), digital certificates for ID verification (Japan, Lithuania), virtual safeboxes for data exchange (Israel), channel encryption (Italy), and IP security and Internet key exchange (Japan). A few respondents also noted data de-identification and pseudonymisation (Italy) and even data anonymisation (Costa Rica).

Respondents reported methods they are using to secure EHR data from unauthorised access, hacking and malware. These include virus scanning, firewalls, controlled access, access logs, audit logs, automated log-out, timely software updates, network separation, auditing hardware and databases, physical security for networked hardware, staff training in data security including how to identify phishing schemes, malware and other malicious programs, penetration tests (ethical hacking), vulnerability scanning, national authorities supervising cybersecurity among data processors, and business continuity and disaster recovery planning.

Principle 12: Organisations to demonstrate meeting national expectations

National health data governance frameworks put in place by Adherents should require organisations processing personal health data to demonstrate that they meet national expectations for health data governance. This may include establishment of certification or accreditation of health data processors.

The 2019-20 OECD survey asked detailed questions about the elements of the Council Recommendation on Health Data Governance to the custodians of 13 key national health datasets. Thus the survey results, which have been fully published, provide a mechanism to identify gaps and differences in the performance of each respondent's most significant organisations managing health and health care data (Oderkirk, 2021[10]).

Most respondents have 3 to 5 different organisations in custody of the 13 key health datasets studied. However, in Ireland and the Netherlands there are 9 different organisations in custody of key national datasets and in France there are 7 different organisations. These respondents have considerably higher challenges integrating and linking data across the pathway of care than in other respondents, as laws and policies governing health data accessibility and sharing would need to be considered and applied across multiple organisations.

In the 2019-20 survey, Australia was the only country who reported that public authorities in must be accredited as an Integrating Authority before they can undertake high risk data integration projects, such as the record linkage of national (Commonwealth) datasets. Accreditation assures that the data integration will take place in a safe and secure manner.

As discussed in this section, more commonly reported were the implementation of laws or regulations that support health data interoperability, the certification of software vendors of electronic health record systems to improve interoperability and quality auditing the content of clinical records.

Legislation requiring adoption of Electronic Health Record Systems that conform to national standards

In the 2021 survey, 18 respondents reported that there are laws or regulations requiring health care providers meet standards for national electronic health record interoperability. Seventeen respondents reported that laws or regulations require electronic messaging standards and 17 respondents reported that there are laws or regulations that require terminology standards.

Table 4.6. Laws or regulations require standards for EHR interoperability

Respondent	Laws or regulations require clinical terminology standards	Laws or regulations require electronic messaging standards	Laws or regulations require health care providers meet standards for national EHR interoperability
Australia	No	No	No
Austria	Yes	Yes	Yes
Belgium	No	No	No
Canada	No[3]	No[3]	No[3]
Costa Rica	Yes	Yes	Yes
Czech Republic	n.r.	n.r.	n.r.
Denmark	No	No	Yes
Estonia	Yes	Yes	Yes
Finland	Yes	Yes	Yes
Germany	n.r.	n.r.	n.r.
Hungary	Yes	Yes	Yes
Iceland	Yes	Yes[1]	Yes
Israel	Yes[2]	No	No
Italy	Yes	Yes	Yes
Japan	Yes	Yes	Yes
Korea	Yes	Yes	Yes
Lithuania	Yes	Yes	Yes
Luxembourg	No	Yes	Yes
Mexico	n.r.	n.r.	n.r.
Netherlands	Yes	No	No
Norway	n.r.	n.r.	Yes
Portugal	No	Yes	No
Russian Federation (non-Adherent)	Yes	Yes	Yes
Slovenia	Yes	Yes	Yes
Sweden	n.r.	n.r.	n.r.
Switzerland	Yes	Yes	Yes
Turkey	Yes	Yes	Yes
United States	Yes[4]	Yes[4]	Yes[5]
Total Yes	17	17	18

Notes: n.r. Not Reported // n.a. Not Applicable // d.k. Unknown.
1. Law recommends the use of EHRs.
2. For diagnosis.
3. Varies among provinces and territories.
4. Office of the National Co-ordinator for Health Information Technology (ONC) rule.
5. Centers for Medicare and Medicaid Services (CMS) rule.
Source: OECD 2021 Survey of Electronic Health Record System Development, Use and Governance.

Certification of Electronic Health Record System Software Vendors

In the 2021 EHR survey, 16 respondents reported that they have a certification process for the vendors of electronic health record system software that requires vendors to conform to particular health information exchange (electronic messaging) standards. Thirteen respondents reported a certification process that requires adherence to national standards for clinical terminology and 13 reported certifying vendors for adherence to requirements or standards for national EHR interoperability.

While not a national certification of software vendors, reimbursement for medical expenditures requires that providers follow certain terminology and exchange requirements in Israel. In Luxembourg, there is a national labelling process for software vendors to access the national EHR system. In Italy, there are no national requirements for certification but individual regions may impose requirements. In Slovenia, certification has been legally authorised but it is not yet implemented due to resource constraints. However, to connect to the national EHR system in Slovenia, vendors must use nationally standardised APIs (Application Programming Interfaces).

Table 4.7. Certification requirements of vendors of EHR system software

Respondent	Conform to particular clinical terminology standards	Conform to particular electronic messaging standards	Conform to national EHR interoperability requirements or standards
Australia	No	Yes	No
Belgium	Yes	Yes	Yes
Canada	No	No[5]	Yes[1]
Costa Rica	No	No	No
Czech Republic	No	No	No
Denmark	Yes	Yes	Yes
Estonia	No	No	No
Finland	Yes	Yes	Yes
Germany	n.r.	n.r.	n.r.
Hungary	Yes	Yes	Yes
Iceland	No	No	No
Israel	No	No	No
Italy	No	No	No
Japan	Yes	Yes	Yes
Korea	Yes	Yes	Yes
Lithuania	No	No	No
Luxembourg	No	No	No
Mexico	n.r.	n.r.	n.r.
Netherlands	Yes	Yes	No
Norway	No	No	No
Portugal	Yes[3]	Yes[3]	Yes[3]
Russian Federation (non-Adherent)	Yes	Yes	Yes
Slovenia	Yes	Yes	Yes
Sweden	No	Yes	No
Switzerland	Yes[2]	Yes[2]	Yes[2]
Turkey	Yes	Yes	Yes
United States	Yes[4]	Yes[4]	Yes[4]
Total yes	13	15	13

Notes: n.r. Not Reported // n.a. Not Applicable // d.k. Unknown.
1. Optional.
2. Certification of communities using EHR software.
3. E-prescription services are certified.
4. Certification is voluntary but required for reimbursement of medical claims from national insurance programmes (Medicare, Medicaid).
5. Varies among provinces and territories.
Source: OECD 2021 Survey of Electronic Health Record System Development, Use and Governance.

Auditing clinical records for quality

Another mechanism to verify if health data meet national expectations for data quality is to conduct audits of clinical records. In the 2021 EHR survey, 13 respondents reported that the electronic clinical records of physicians, medical specialists and hospitals are audited to verify quality. An additional three respondents indicated that at least one of these three groups are audited to verify quality. In most cases, it is a national authority that is responsible for undertaking quality audits. In Canada and Sweden, regional authorities conduct audits. In Switzerland, private sector organisations can be certified to then conduct audits as part of certifying the compliance of communities to national requirements including auditing clinical records for quality. Under law in the United States, health care providers are responsible for generating auditing reports on the quality of their clinical records and ensuring data quality.

Table 4.8. Auditing of electronic health records for quality

Respondent	Physicians	Medical specialists	Hospitals	All
Australia	Yes	Yes	Yes	Yes
Belgium	No	No	Yes	Yes
Canada	Yes	Yes	Yes	Yes
Costa Rica	Yes	Yes	Yes	Yes
Czech Republic	No	No	No	No
Denmark	Yes	Yes	n.r.	Yes
Estonia	No	No	No	No
Finland	n.r.	n.r.	n.r.	n.r.
Germany	n.r.	n.r.	n.r.	n.r.
Hungary	Yes	Yes	Yes	Yes
Iceland	Yes	Yes	Yes	Yes
Israel	Yes	Yes	Yes	Yes
Italy	n.r.	n.r.	n.r.	n.r.
Japan	n.r.	n.r.	n.r.	n.r.
Korea	No	No	No	No
Lithuania	No	No	No	No
Luxembourg	No	No	No	No
Mexico	Yes	Yes	Yes	Yes
Netherlands	Yes	Yes	Yes	Yes
Norway	n.r.	n.r.	n.r.	n.r.
Portugal	Yes	n.r.	Yes	n.r.
Russian Federation (non-Adherent)	Yes	Yes	Yes	Yes
Slovenia	No	No	No	No
Sweden	Yes	Yes	Yes	Yes
Switzerland	Yes	Yes	Yes	Yes
Turkey	Yes	Yes	Yes	Yes
United States	Yes	Yes	Yes	Yes
Total yes	15	14	15	13

Note: n.r. Not Reported // n.a. Not Applicable // d.k. Unknown.
Source: OECD 2021 Survey of Electronic Health Record System Development, Use and Governance.

Second recommendation: Transborder co-operation

The second recommendation provides that Adherents should support transborder co-operation in the processing of personal health data for health system management, research, statistics and other health related purposes subject to safeguards. Governments should identify and remove barriers to cross-border co-operation in the processing of personal health data, facilitate the interoperability of health data governance frameworks, and promote continuous improvement through the sharing of outcomes and best practices in the availability and use of personal health data for purposes that serve the public interest.

In the 2019-20 survey, respondents surveyed were asked to report recent policy relevant projects involving multiple countries in the linkage of their datasets or in the extraction of data from clinical record systems. These projects include parallel studies, where researchers in each country followed a common study protocol, and studies where data were shared across borders. The projects reported by Adherents included studies of prescription drug use and harms between Australia and Canada; between the United States and Canada; among Denmark, Finland, Norway and Sweden; and among Australia, United States, Denmark, Finland, Iceland, Norway and Sweden. There are examples of indicator development and research to improve health system performance including projects between Latvia and Slovenia; among Japan and other countries in Asia; and among Finland, Hungary, Italy, the Netherlands, Norway, United Kingdom (Scotland) and Sweden. There were multiple examples of global and European projects examining cancer incidence and survival; and multiple examples of European projects involving indicator development and research.

Data localisation laws and policies create obstacles to cross border projects

Data protection and privacy frameworks generally apply conditions to the transfer of health data for research purposes abroad, seeking to continue to guarantee a high level of protection to the transferred data (Magazanik, 2022[9]). In this respect, discussions often arise with respect to the relationship between data protection and privacy frameworks and 'data localisation' requirements, i.e. whether the requirements data privacy laws impose on transborder personal data flows amount to a form of data localisation.

There is not yet a universally accepted definition of what data localisation is. However, drawing upon a range of definitions, the OECD has recently proposed the following understanding:

> " *Data localisation refers to a mandatory legal or administrative requirement directly or indirectly stipulating that data be stored or processed, exclusively ('data copy cannot leave') or non-exclusively ('data copy must stay'), within a specified jurisdiction (Svantesson, 2020[30]).*"

This definition of data localisation distinguishes between conditions imposed on transborder data transfers and 'bans' on transborder data transfers. The data localisation requirement in line with this definition is about mandating of location, with focus being placed on data to be stored or processed on physical servers or digital storage units within a specified jurisdiction. This is a distinct and separate matter from requirements relating to a prescribed level of protection, such as a data protection or cyber security standards that may be imposed for the purpose of achieving legitimate privacy objectives as a condition for transborder data transfers.

Measures that may persuade an organisation to locate their data in a particular jurisdiction are relatively widespread for the purpose of achieving legitimate objectives such as protection of personal data, cybersecurity, law enforcement, and national security, as well as ensuring access to certain categories of data that are viewed as particularly sensitive or closely tied to an important governmental interest. In general, the requirements data privacy laws traditionally impose on transborder data transfers do not necessarily amount to data localisation (Svantesson, 2020[30]).

Nonetheless, in some OECD countries, data localisation regimes either explicitly forbid health data processors from approving the sharing of data with an organisation located outside of their country or create obstacles such as a lack of clarity about how health data sharing outside of the border might be approved (Svantesson, 2020[30]).

Existing privacy regimes can also result in processes to obtain approval for health data transfers that would be prohibitive in terms of time and resources. In federated countries, laws and policies within states, provinces or regions may entrench data localisation at a national level.

In the 2019-20 survey, Adherents were asked if de-identified data from key national health datasets may be shared with approved researchers working in a foreign academic or non-profit research organisation. Seven countries, Australia, Belgium, Denmark, Finland, Norway, Singapore and Slovenia reported that de-identified data from all health care datasets could be shared for approved research to take place outside of their country. Another six countries reported sharing data outside of their country was possible with the majority of health care datasets. A minority of de-identified health care datasets could be shared cross-border in Austria and Latvia.

Australia noted that while such sharing is possible, it would only be permitted for health data that cannot be re-identified and no instances of such sharing are known in practice. Australian researchers who demonstrate that their work has been approved by the appropriate ethics committee should be able to access de-identified data securely. However, approval processes can be complex and lengthy in order to ensure that the use of the data would be secure and appropriate. This results in practice to limitations in the access and use of these data.

Canada reported that such sharing is possible at the national level but only if it is not prohibited by provincial law or by the terms of data sharing agreements with data suppliers. Similarly, Germany also indicated that due to the federal structure, local state data protection laws and laws governing hospitals may prohibit data sharing with foreign entities within, and outside of, national borders. This illustrates how the harmonisation of policy frameworks within countries is critical.

Cancer registry data are the national data that are the most likely to be shared internationally. Fourteen countries reported that they could share de-identified national cancer registry data with approved foreign researchers in academic and non-profit organisations. Along with the rich history of international cancer research collaboration, this reflects the success of creating a policy and legislative environment that enables relevant data to be available for research. It also illustrates that it is possible to share de-identified personal health data for secondary uses with the requisite political will and co-ordination of effort.

In some countries, however, no key national de-identified health care data can be shared with foreign researchers. Eight countries, the Czech Republic, Ireland, Israel, Japan, Korea, Sweden, United Kingdom (Scotland) and the United States, would not approve sharing de-identified data from any of the 13 key national health datasets with a foreign researcher in the academic or non-profit sectors. The United States generally does not restrict international transfers of data, but extra-territorial risks to privacy compliance must be considered (Magazanik, 2022[9]). The United States reported that while there is no access to de-identified person-level national health care datasets (restricted datasets) for foreign researchers, some research needs of foreign researchers may be met through access to public-use microdata files, which are datasets where variables have been processed and treated to ensure a very low re-identification risk.

Table 4.9. Foreign academic and non-profit researchers may be approved access to de-identified personal health data in some countries

Potential for access approval to 10 key national de-identified health care datasets

Respondent	Hospital in-patient data	Mental hospital in-patient data	Emergency health care data	Primary care data	Prescription medicines data	Cancer registry data	Diabetes registry data	Cardio-vascular disease registry data	Mortality data	Formal long-term care data	% of national health care datasets
Australia	Yes[1]	Yes[1]	Yes[1]	Yes[1]	Yes[1]	Yes[1]	Yes[1]	n.a.	Yes[1]	Yes[1]	100%
Austria	Yes	No	No	No	No	Yes	n.a.	No	Yes	No	33%
Belgium	Yes	Yes	Yes	Yes	Yes[3]	Yes	Yes	n.a.	n.a.	n.a.	100%
Canada	Yes[2]	Yes[2]	Yes[2]	n.r.	No	Yes	n.a.	n.a.	Yes[4]	Yes[2]	75%
Czech Republic	No	No	No	n.a.	No	No	No	No	No	n.a.	0%
Denmark	Yes	Yes	Yes	Yes	Yes	Yes	Yes	Yes	Yes	Yes	100%
Estonia	Yes	Yes	Yes	Yes	Yes	Yes	n.a.	No	Yes	Yes	89%
Finland	Yes[7]	Yes[7]	Yes[7]	Yes[7]	Yes[7]	Yes[7]	n.a.	Yes[7]	Yes[7]	Yes[7]	100%
France	Yes	Yes	Yes	Yes	Yes	No	n.a.	No	Yes	Yes	78%
Germany	Yes	n.a.	n.a.	n.a.	No	Yes	n.a.	n.a.	n.a.	n.a.	67%
Ireland	n.r.	n.r.	n.r.	n.a.	n.r.	n.r.	n.a.	n.a.	n.r.	n.r.	0%
Israel	No	No	No	No	n.a.	No	No	n.a.	No	No	0%
Japan	No	No	No	No	No	No	n.a.	n.a.	No	No	0%
Korea	No	No	No	No	No	No	No	n.a.	No	No	0%
Latvia	No	No	No	No	No	Yes	Yes	n.a.	Yes	n.a.	38%
Luxembourg	Yes[5]	Yes[5]	n.a.	No	No	Yes	n.a.	n.a.	Yes[6]	No	57%
Netherlands	No	No	Yes	Yes	Yes	Yes	No	Yes	Yes	No	60%
Norway	Yes	Yes	Yes	Yes	Yes	Yes	Yes	Yes	Yes	Yes	100%
Singapore (non-Adherent)	Yes	Yes	Yes	Yes	Yes	Yes	Yes	Yes	Yes	Yes	100%
Slovenia	Yes	Yes	Yes	Yes	Yes	Yes	n.a.	n.a.	Yes	n.a.	100%
Sweden	No	No	No	n.a.	No	No	No	No	No	No	0%
United Kingdom (Scotland)	No	No	No	No	No	No	No	No	No	No	0%
United States	No	n.r.	No	No	No	n.r.	n.r.	n.r.	No	No	0%

Notes: n.a.: not applicable; n.r.: not reported; d.k.: unknown.
1. Potentially yes, but only if the data cannot be re-identified and we are unaware of any arrangements to date.
2. Except where prohibited by law or agreement.
3. Data without risk of re-identification.
4. Data is shared with WHO.
5. Yes for the dataset of National Health Insurance and the Directorate of Health.
6. Data is shared with Eurostat.
7. Subject to permission.
Source: Oderkirk (2021[10]), "Survey Results: National Health Data Infrastructure and Governance", https://doi.org/10.1787/55d24b5d-en.

On the 2019-20 survey, Israel reported that privacy policies limit approval of data sharing outside of the country, but mechanisms exist to permit sharing under agreed conditions. The preference, however, is to provide access to information/research results.

Under the European General Data Protection Regulation (GDPR), de-identified microdata may still be considered personal data and be subject to protection. Because remote access to de-identified personal data is considered a transfer under the GDPR, the regulation's restrictions on cross-border data transfers apply to many available mechanisms to provide foreign bone fide researchers with access to health data for approved research or statistics (Magazanik, 2022[9]). Ensuring that GDPR requirements are met was noted in the 2019/20 survey as a barrier to data sharing by Germany and the Netherlands.

Third recommendation: Data exchange and interoperability

The third recommendation provides that governments should engage with relevant experts and organisations to develop mechanisms consistent with this Recommendation that enable the efficient exchange and interoperability of health data while protecting privacy and including, where appropriate, codes, standards and the standardisation of health data terminology.

As was discussed earlier, there is a wide variety of national and international terminology standards used by respondents. In 2021, 17 respondents reported using the HL7 FHIR standard which provides a modern approach to interoperability and could help to address problems within countries of the use of multiple standards for the same terms. To the extent that there is global collaboration in the development and implementation of FHIR Application Programming Interfaces (APIs), there is potential for this standard to facilitate standardisation globally.

Encouragingly, respondents reported participation in global collaborative work toward agreed international standards for clinical terminology and data exchange (electronic messaging). In 2021, 15 respondents reported participating in the Integrating the Health care Enterprise International collaboration and 10 respondents reported participating in the Global Digital Health Partnership (Table 4.10).

There is extensive work underway within the European Union (EU) toward improving the accessibility, sharing and use of health data that, if successful, would have an influence on the evolution of global collaboration in the sharing, use and protection of health data. A key EU project is the eHealth Digital Service Infrastructure (eHDSI) for cross-border health data exchange under the Connecting Europe Facility (CEF) that is supporting EHR data exchange at the country level and the provision of core services at the EU level. Another key project is the Joint Action Towards the European Health Data Space (TEHDAS). TEHDAS is developing European principles for the secondary use of health data, building upon successful development of health data hubs in a few countries, such as France and Finland, and aiming to develop health data governance and rules for cross-border data exchange, improve data quality and provide strong technical infrastructure and interoperability (EC, 2021[31]). The European Health Data Space has the potential to act as a powerful federator between national data hubs, promoting interoperability standards, best practices for data sharing across the European Union and setting a coherent governance framework.

Table 4.10. Global collaborations for exchange and terminology standards

Respondents	IHE (Integrating the Health care Enterprise) International	Global Digital Health Partnership	EU projects to facilitate sharing and utilising EHR data across EU member states
Australia	No	Yes	No
Austria	Yes	Yes	Yes
Belgium	Yes	No	Yes
Canada	n.r.	Yes	No
Costa Rica	No	No	No
Czech Republic	Yes	n.r.	Yes
Denmark	Yes	No	Yes
Estonia	Yes	Yes	Yes
Finland	Yes	No	Yes
Germany	n.r.	n.r.	Yes
Hungary	No	No	Yes
Iceland	No	No	Yes
Israel	No	No	n.a.
Italy	No	No	Yes
Japan	Yes	Yes	No
Korea	No	Yes	No
Lithuania	Yes	No	Yes
Luxembourg	Yes	No	Yes
Mexico	n.r.	n.r.	n.r.
Netherlands	Yes	Yes	Yes
Norway	n.r.	n.r.	Yes
Portugal	Yes	Yes	Yes
Russian Federation (non-Adherent)	n.r.	n.r.	n.r.
Slovenia	No	No	Yes
Sweden	Yes	No	Yes
Switzerland	Yes	Yes	No
Turkey	Yes	No	Yes
United States	Yes	Yes	No
Total Yes	15	10	18

Notes: n.r. Not Reported // n.a. Not Applicable // d.k. Unknown.
Source: OECD 2021 Survey of Electronic Health Record System Development, Use and Governance.

The 2021 survey also asked respondents about the coding of health data to common data models which facilitate within country statistical and research projects. In 2021, five respondents reported coding data within their EHR systems to a common data model. When the common data model is international in scope, such as the OMOP (Observational Medical Outcomes Partnership) common data model, such coding efforts support internationally comparable data for a wide array of research and statistical uses. There were some applications of the OMOP reported by Australia and Israel in 2021. As was discussed in the section on Principle 11, HIRA in Korea coded linked health data, including HIRA's national insurance claims data, for the purposes of encouraging secure access to timely data for global COVID-19 research as part of the OHDISI project. France is coding data within the Health Data Hub to the OMOP common data model as part of the EHDEN project.

5 Summary and conclusions

Implementation

The Recommendation provides a roadmap toward more harmonised approaches to health data governance across Adherents. Overall results of this Report indicate that there are many Adherents that are still working toward implementation (Figure 5.1). Among Adherents with lower scores for dataset availability, maturity and use, the challenge lies in making data available for research and statistical purposes and there is work to be done to develop collaborative policies and practices among government authorities in custody of key health data and considerable work and investments required to improve data quality, linkability and sharing with researchers so that data can serve the health-related public interest. Among Adherents with lower scores for dataset governance, there are gaps to address in data privacy and security protections for key health datasets such as having a data protection officer and providing staff training, access controls, managing re-identification risks, and protecting data when they are linked and accessed.

The 2019-20 survey identified a small cluster of Adherents with policies, regulations and practices that foster the development, use, accessibility and sharing of key national health datasets for research and statistical purposes while also having a high degree of recommended health data governance policies and practices in place. Adherents reporting the strongest national health data availability, maturity and use and health dataset governance policies and practices were Denmark, Finland, and Korea. These countries were followed by Australia, Canada, France, Latvia, the Netherlands, Slovenia, Sweden and the United Kingdom (Scotland).

Figure 5.1. Small group of Adherents score highly on both dataset availability, maturity and use and dataset governance

Dataset governance score, max=15

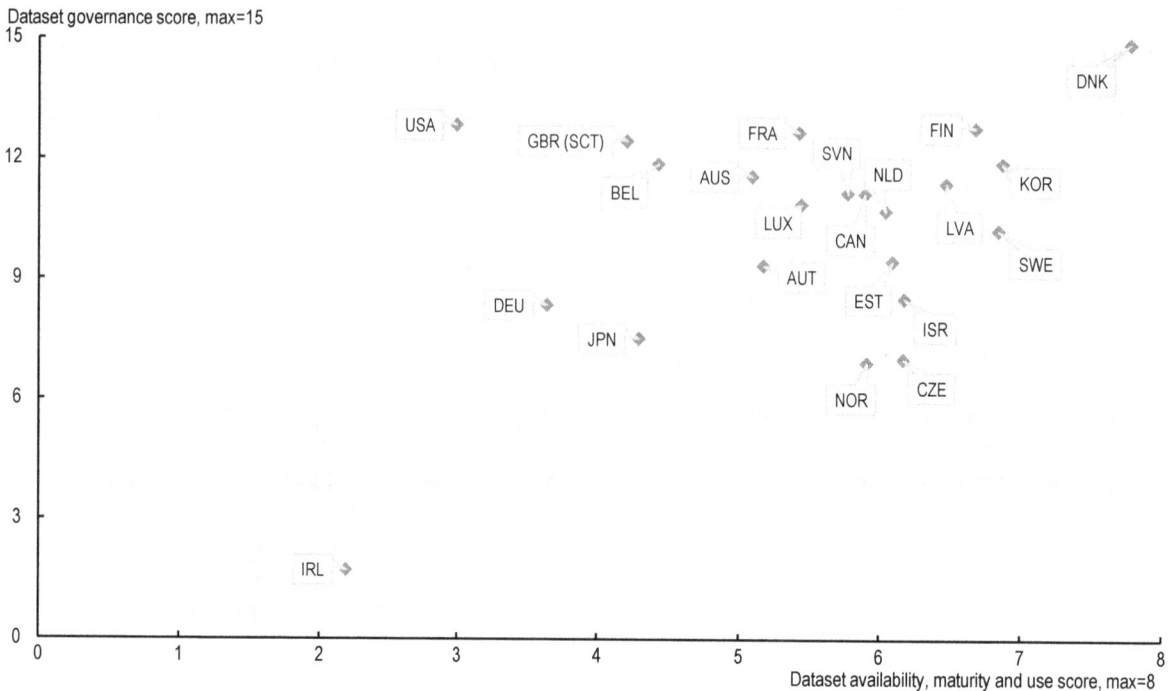

Note: Dataset governance score is the sum or the proportion of health care datasets meeting 15 dataset governance elements and the dataset availability, maturity and use score is the sum of the proportion of health datasets meeting 8 elements of dataset availability maturity and use. See Annex B Tables A.1 and A.2.
Source: Oderkirk (2021[10]), "Survey Results: National Health Data Infrastructure and Governance", https://doi.org/10.1787/55d24b5d-en.

All respondents experienced some challenges and difficulties in developing national health data governance frameworks. The most commonly experienced challenges were legal restrictions or policy barriers to public authorities undertaking data linkages (16 respondents); concerns with the quality of data that limit their usefulness (15 respondents); and legal restrictions or policy barriers to sharing data among public authorities (13 respondents).

The 2021 survey of Electronic Health Record System Development, Data Use and Governance revealed both shortcomings in the implementation of standards for clinical terminology and the interoperability of health data and emerging solutions including new standards, global collaborative efforts toward global standards and the adoption of common data models. Health data interoperability will remain a significant challenge for the sector in the coming years.

Priorities for further work that emerged from the January 2021 OECD-Israel workshop discussions included the following:

- Insufficient clarity and harmonisation between national health data governance frameworks challenge their implementation within nations and between them.
- Data localisation laws and policies limit cross-border collaboration in health research.
- Conflicts about the appropriate legal basis for data processing: Consent vs. Public Interest – and the scope of "Public interest" – affect countries' ability to conduct research and streamline data sharing project approvals.

- Insufficient awareness of and expertise in the use of Privacy Enhancing Solutions limit their wider adoption to strengthen data protection and limit their consideration when developing legal basis for data processing or approving data processing requests.
- Necessity of fostering public trust of individuals, communities and societies in scientific research that is in the public interest, through Inclusion, Transparency and Participation.
- Importance of recognising and addressing inequalities in access to data for research, such as when researchers from diverse backgrounds are denied access to data due to payment or credit sharing requirements, and the risks of bias in research results emanating from this.
- Importance of recognising and addressing the consequences of inequalities emanating from potential bias in the data explored, in and of itself, or due to insufficient inclusion of participants from diverse populations.
- Necessity of strong digital identification methods on a national level to support data linkage whilst preserving privacy and security.
- These priorities are consistent with the Recommendation and point to further work that the OECD can do to support implementation of the Recommendation and the monitoring of its impact.

Dissemination

Overall, the Recommendation has been widely disseminated to various stakeholders through various avenues, including in the context of the publication of a booklet introducing and presenting the Recommendation; academic publications, articles and reports; workshops, meetings and bilateral discussions; surveys, policy briefs and country reviews regarding health information systems and governance (OECD, 2019[7]). The Recommendation has also been shared in the context of other international fora including the G7 Health Ministers as they focussed on international collaboration in health data in 2021; the World Health Organization Global Summit on Health Data Governance in June 2021; meetings of the Health Data Co-operative in 2021; and the G20 Digital Health Taskforce in 2020 work on digital health interventions for pandemic management.

Key points from this Report will be published as a policy toolkit on health data governance to be disseminated as part of the Going Digital Project series of policy toolkits. Aspects of this Report will also inform the Going Digital III Project on Data Governance reports in 2022 on Tangible Responses and Recovery from the COVID-19 Pandemic; on Data Stewardship, Access and Control; and the Report from this horizontal project on Data Governance. Results of this Report will also inform work of the Health Committee to support greater resilience to public health crisis among health systems; as well as further work in future years to support countries in strengthening their health information systems and the governance of health data.

Other international organisations have recently begun engaging in work toward supporting the cross-country harmonisation of health data and governance and this Recommendation has made an important contribution to their work. This includes recent efforts by the WHO, the EU, the G7, the G20 and the Lancet Commission. The OECD's continued contributions to the health data governance work of other international bodies helps to assure this Recommendation has a broad impact.

The focus of Adherents over the past five years has been on the implementation of the recommendation at the national level. In the next five years, Adherents are encouraged to disseminate the Recommendation to other levels of government and to non-governmental organisations.

Continued relevance

The health sector remains significantly behind other economic sectors such as transportation, travel, banking and finance, in the interoperability of data. The Recommendation was designed to be technology neutral and robust to the evolution of health data and health data technologies.

The Recommendation has been particularly important because of the global COVID-19 pandemic. The pandemic shone a spotlight on the capacity of each countries' health information systems to provide critical information for the public welfare; as well as on aspects of data governance that created obstacles to responding to the pandemic in a timely way. As was discussed in the section on dissemination, the Secretariat is increasingly in demand to present the Recommendation and our findings regarding progress toward its implementation at meetings of international organisations and conferences and to provide support to countries in the review and advancement of their health information systems. Further, the Recommendation and this draft Report are contributing to a new OECD Going Digital III horizontal project to support countries in strengthening data governance and thus is proving its worth to sectors beyond health.

Next steps

It is proposed that the Health Committee and the Committee on Digital Economy Policy continue to support and report to Council on the implementation, dissemination and continued relevance of the Recommendation for another 5 years. This next report could monitor progress in the implementation of the Recommendation through the continuation of the HCQO surveys of the development, use and governance of key health data and health data governance. Further, the OECD should continue the new series of country reviews of health information systems to support countries in their efforts to develop health data governance.

Work could focus on some of the priorities areas that emerged from the January 2021 OECD-Israel workshop discussions, and in particular on three areas that pose challenges for Adherents in implementing the Recommendation and would support Adherents in achieving health information systems that are inclusive and support greater resilience to shocks: 1) increasing the interoperability of health data and data analytics; 2) achieving greater harmonisation of health data governance frameworks for cross-country collaboration involving the sharing and use of health data; and 3) enhancing the sharing of experiences and best practices in health data security in response to the increasing occurrence of malicious attacks on health data.

The CDEP through its subsidiary bodies, will also continue to explore the aforementioned issues and challenges. More specifically, through its work on measures that condition the movement of data across borders, on the economic and societal consequences of these measures, and as it continues to develop further practical guidance in areas such as privacy enhancing technologies, regulatory sandboxes, and digital security risk management. Further, the CDEP will continue to monitor and examine approaches to data access and sharing, data-enabled competition and market concentration; as well as improved measurement of data, data usage and exchange.

Adherents should also be encouraged to continue implementing the Recommendation and to further disseminate the Recommendation at all levels of government as well as to other stakeholders such as non-governmental organisations involved in processing personal health data. Assessment by Adherents of the impact of their national health data governance framework on the availability and use of personal health data could help them to identify areas where they need to enhance their efforts to implement the Recommendation.

References

Alder, S. (2021), *2020 Healthcare Data Breach Report: 25% Increase in Breaches in 2020*, https://www.hipaajournal.com/2020-healthcare-data-breach-report-us/. [24]

Anderson, G. and J. Oderkirk (eds.) (2015), *Dementia Research and Care: Can Big Data Help?*, OECD Publishing, Paris, https://doi.org/10.1787/9789264228429-en. [4]

Andreux, M. (2020), "Federated Survival Analysis with Discrete-Time Cox Models, International Workshop on Federated Learning for User Privacy and Data Confidentiality in Conjunction with ICML 2020 (FL-ICML'20)", *Machine Learning*, https://doi.org/10.48550/arXiv.2006.08997. [27]

BakerHostetler (2019), *Managing Enterprise Risks in a Digital World*, Baker Hostetler, US, https://f.datasrvr.com/fr1/419/17257/2019_BakerHostetler_DSIR_Final.pdf?cbcachex=990603. [23]

Canada (2021), "Pan-Canadian Health Data Strategy, Expert Advisory Group Report 1: Charting a Path Toward Ambition,", https://www.canada.ca/en/public-health/corporate/mandate/about-agency/external-advisory-bodies/list/pan-canadian-health-data-strategy-report. [21]

Di Iorio, C. (2019), "Assessing data protection and governance in health information systems: a novel methodology of Privacy and Ethics Impact and Performance Assessment (PEIPA)", *J Med Ethics*, https://doi.org/10.1136/medethics-201. [15]

Di Iorio, C., F. Carinci and J. Oderkirk (2013), "Health research and systems' governance are at risk: should the right to data protection override health?", *Journal of Medical Ethics*, Vol. 40/7, pp. 488-492, https://doi.org/10.1136/medethics-2013-101603. [5]

EC (2021), *e-Health Digital Health and Care - European Health Data Space*, https://ec.europa.eu/health/ehealth/dataspace_en. [31]

EHDEN (2021), *European Health Data and Evidence Network*, https://www.ehden.eu/. [26]

Eichler, H. (2019), "Data Rich, Information Poor: Can We Use Electronic Health Records to Create a Learning Healthcare System for Pharmaceuticals?", *Clin Pharmacol Ther*, Vol. 105/4, pp. 912-922, https://pubmed.ncbi.nlm.nih.gov/30178490/. [14]

Haring R, K. (ed.) (2020), *Health Information Systems, Electronic Medical Records, and Big Data in Global Healthcare: Progress and Challenges in OECD Countries*. [13]

Iwaya, S., E. Koksal-Oudot and E. Ronchi (2021), "Promoting comparability in personal data breach notification reporting", *OECD Digital Economy Papers*, No. 322, OECD Publishing, Paris, https://doi.org/10.1787/88f79eb0-en. [22]

Magazanik, L. (2022), *Supporting Health Innovation With Fair Information Practice Principles: Key issues emerging from the OECD-Israel Workshop of 19-20 January 2021*, OECD, https://www.oecd.org/health/OECD-Israel-Health-Data-Governance-Workshop-Report.pdf. [9]

NHS Digital (2021), "Trusted Research Environment Service for England", https://digital.nhs.uk/coronavirus/coronavirus-data-services-updates/trusted-research-environment-service-for-england#working-in-the-safe-setting-nhs-digital-s-data-access-environment. [28]

Oderkirk, J. (2021), "Survey results: National health data infrastructure and governance", *OECD Health Working Papers*, No. 127, OECD Publishing, Paris, https://doi.org/10.1787/55d24b5d-en. [10]

Oderkirk, J. (2018), "Governing data for better health and healthcare", *OECD Observer*, http://OECD Observer. [11]

Oderkirk, J. (2017), "Readiness of electronic health record systems to contribute to national health information and research", *OECD Health Working Papers*, No. 99, OECD Publishing, Paris, https://doi.org/10.1787/9e296bf3-en. [3]

Oderkirk, J., E. Ronchi and N. Klazinga (2013), "International comparisons of health system performance among OECD countries: Opportunities and data privacy protection challenges", *Health Policy*, Vol. 112/1-2, pp. 9-18, https://doi.org/10.1016/j.healthpol.2013.06.006. [6]

OECD (2022), *Towards an Integrated Health Information System in the Netherlands*, OECD Publishing, Paris, https://doi.org/10.1787/a1568975-en. [20]

OECD (2021), *OECD Going Digital Toolkit: Trust Dimension*, OECD, Paris, https://goingdigital.oecd.org/dimension/trust. [18]

OECD (2020), *OECD Policy Responses to Coronavirus (COVID-19)*, OECD Publishing, Paris, https://www.oecd.org/coronavirus/en/policy-responses. [19]

OECD (2020), "Opportunities and challenges in blockchain technologies in health care", *OECD Blockchain Policy Series*, OECD, Paris, https://www.oecd.org/finance/Opportunities-and-Challenges-of-Blockchain-Technologies-in-Health-Care.pdf. [17]

OECD (2019), *Health in the 21st Century: Putting Data to Work for Stronger Health Systems*, OECD Health Policy Studies, OECD Publishing, Paris, https://doi.org/10.1787/e3b23f8e-en. [12]

OECD (2019), "Recommendation of the Council on Health Data Governance", OECD Publishing, http://www.oecd.org/health/health-systems/Recommendation-of-OECD-Council-on-Health-Data-Governance-Booklet.pdf. [7]

OECD (2017), "Ministerial Statement", *OECD Health Ministerial Meeting: The Next Generation of Health Reforms*, OECD, Paris, https://www.oecd.org/health/ministerial-statement-2017.pdf. [8]

OECD (2015), *Health Data Governance: Privacy, Monitoring and Research*, OECD Health Policy Studies, OECD Publishing, Paris, https://doi.org/10.1787/9789264244566-en. [2]

OECD (2013), *Strengthening Health Information Infrastructure for Health Care Quality Governance: Good Practices, New Opportunities and Data Privacy Protection Challenges*, OECD Health Policy Studies, OECD Publishing, Paris, https://doi.org/10.1787/9789264193505-en. [1]

Oliveira Hashiguchi, T., L. Slawomirski and J. Oderkirk (2021), "Laying the foundations for artificial intelligence in health", *OECD Health Working Papers*, No. 128, OECD Publishing, Paris, https://doi.org/10.1787/3f62817d-en. [16]

OpenSAFELY (2021), *Secure analytics platform for NHS Electronic Health Records*, https://www.opensafely.org/. [29]

Raisaro, J. (2020), "SCOR: A secure international informatics infrastructure to investigate COVID-19", *Journal of the American Medical Informatics Association*, Vol. 27/11, pp. 1721-1726, https://doi.org/10.1093/jamia/ocaa172. [25]

Svantesson, D. (2020), "Data localisation trends and challenges: Considerations for the review of the Privacy Guidelines", *OECD Digital Economy Papers*, No. 301, OECD Publishing, Paris, https://doi.org/10.1787/7fbaed62-en. [30]

Annex A. Supplementary tables

Table A A.1. Key national health dataset availability, maturity and use

Country	% of key national health datasets available[1]	% of available health care datasets with coverage of 80% or more of the population	% of available health care datasets where data extracted automatically from electronic clinical or administrative records	% of available health datasets where the time between record creation and inclusion in the dataset is one week or less	% of available health datasets sharing the same unique patient ID	% of available health care datasets where standard codes are used for clinical terminology	% of available health datasets used to regularly report on health care quality or health system performance (published indicators)	% of available health datasets regularly linked for research, statistics and/or monitoring (indicators)	Sum
Australia	92%	100%	56%	17%	17%	78%	83%	67%	5.09
Austria	92%	100%	78%	0%	33%	89%	75%	42%	5.17
Belgium	69%	71%	86%	11%	22%	71%	78%	33%	4.42
Canada	85%	75%	75%	0%	64%	100%	91%	100%	5.89
Czech Republic	77%	100%	100%	0%	90%	100%	90%	60%	6.17
Denmark	100%	100%	100%	77%	100%	100%	100%	100%	7.77
Estonia	92%	89%	78%	50%	83%	100%	92%	25%	6.09
Finland	85%	100%	56%	36%	100%	100%	91%	100%	6.67
France	92%	78%	56%	8%	58%	100%	83%	67%	5.42
Germany	31%	100%	33%	0%	0%	100%	100%	0%	3.64
Ireland	77%	86%	29%	0%	0%	29%	0%	0%	2.20
Israel	85%	88%	100%	18%	64%	100%	100%	64%	6.18
Japan	85%	100%	75%	0%	45%	88%	27%	9%	4.29
Korea	92%	89%	89%	58%	100%	100%	92%	67%	6.87
Latvia	77%	88%	63%	80%	80%	100%	90%	70%	6.47
Luxembourg	77%	100%	71%	10%	70%	86%	100%	30%	5.44
Netherlands	92%	70%	100%	0%	75%	100%	83%	83%	6.04
Norway	100%	80%	90%	0%	77%	90%	85%	69%	5.91
Singapore (non-Adherent)	100%	80%	100%	0%	62%	90%	31%	31%	4.93
Slovenia	77%	100%	100%	0%	70%	100%	70%	60%	5.77
Sweden	92%	100%	100%	8%	92%	100%	100%	92%	6.84
United Kingdom (Scotland)	92%	100%	67%	0%	0%	78%	67%	17%	4.20
United States	54%	33%	17%	0%	14%	67%	57%	57%	2.99

Note: The sum column is the sum of the preceding columns and the maximum is 8. n.a: not applicable

1.Thirteen national datasets including ten health care datasets (hospital in-patient, mental hospital in-patient, emergency health care, primary care, prescription medicines, cancer, diabetes, cardiovascular disease, mortality and formal long-term care); patient experiences survey, population health survey and population census/registry.

Source: Oderkirk (2021[10]), "Survey Results: National Health Data Infrastructure and Governance", https://doi.org/10.1787/55d24b5d-en.

Table A A.2. Proportion of key national health care datasets with recommended governance elements

Country	Legislation authorises datasets	Data privacy/data protection officer	Staff are trained in data protection	Staff data access controls	Data de-identified prior to analysis	Testing re-identification attack risk	Data shared within public sector	Data shared with academic/ non-profit sector	Data shared with for-profit sector	Data shared cross-border	Standard data sharing agreement	Either remote data access service or research data centre	Public description of dataset	Description includes legal basis for the dataset	Procedure to request and approval criteria for data linkage are publicly available	Sum
Australia	67%	100%	100%	100%	100%	0%	78%	89%	89%	100%	78%	33%	100%	22%	100%	11.56
Austria	100%	100%	100%	100%	100%	0%	89%	44%	33%	33%	0%	78%	78%	78%	0%	9.33
Belgium	100%	100%	100%	100%	100%	43%	57%	100%	0%	100%	100%	29%	100%	100%	57%	11.86
Canada	25%	100%	100%	100%	100%	0%	88%	88%	75%	75%	88%	25%	88%	75%	88%	11.13
Czech Republic	100%	100%	100%	100%	100%	0%	0%	0%	0%	0%	0%	0%	100%	100%	0%	7.00
Denmark	100%	100%	100%	100%	100%	90%	100%	100%	100%	100%	100%	100%	100%	100%	100%	14.90
Estonia	100%	100%	33%	100%	100%	0%	100%	89%	89%	89%	0%	0%	100%	33%	11%	9.44
Finland	100%	100%	100%	67%	100%	0%	100%	100%	100%	100%	100%	11%	100%	100%	100%	12.78
France	78%	100%	100%	100%	100%	78%	100%	100%	78%	78%	67%	67%	89%	67%	67%	12.67
Germany	67%	67%	33%	33%	67%	33%	33%	67%	33%	67%	67%	33%	100%	100%	33%	8.33
Ireland	100%	14%	14%	0%	0%	0%	0%	0%	0%	0%	14%	0%	14%	0%	14%	1.71
Israel	88%	100%	0%	0%	100%	0%	88%	88%	0%	0%	100%	63%	63%	63%	100%	8.50
Japan	100%	100%	13%	75%	88%	0%	0%	88%	13%	0%	75%	0%	100%	13%	88%	7.50
Korea	100%	100%	100%	100%	100%	89%	89%	89%	0%	0%	78%	78%	89%	89%	89%	11.89
Latvia	100%	100%	100%	100%	100%	0%	100%	100%	0%	38%	100%	0%	100%	100%	100%	11.38
Luxembourg	100%	100%	100%	100%	100%	14%	100%	100%	0%	57%	100%	86%	57%	57%	14%	10.86
Netherlands	80%	100%	100%	60%	100%	20%	70%	80%	20%	60%	100%	50%	100%	70%	60%	10.70
Norway	90%	0%	0%	0%	0%	0%	100%	100%	100%	100%	0%	0%	100%	100%	0%	6.90
Singapore (non-Adherent)	40%	100%	100%	100%	70%	80%	10%	100%	100%	100%	50%	100%	20%	20%	0%	9.90
Slovenia	100%	100%	100%	100%	100%	0%	14%	100%	0%	100%	100%	100%	100%	100%	0%	11.14
Sweden	89%	100%	100%	11%	100%	11%	89%	89%	0%	0%	100%	11%	100%	100%	100%	10.22
United Kingdom (Scotland)	89%	89%	89%	89%	89%	89%	89%	89%	89%	0%	89%	89%	89%	89%	89%	12.44
United States[1]	100%	100%	100%	100%	100%	100%	83%	100%	100%	0%	100%	100%	100%	17%	83%	12.83

Note: The sum is the addition of the preceding columns and the maximum sum is 15.

1. National health care datasets of the US National Centre for Health Statistics.

Source: Oderkirk, (2021[10]), "Survey Results: National Health Data Infrastructure and Governance", https://doi.org/10.1787/55d24b5d-en.

Notes

[1] See Annex A, Table A.A.1 within Oderkirk (2021[10]) for the names, positions and organisations of the persons who co-ordinated the completion of the questionnaire within each country.

[2] The Global Privacy Assembly is a global forum for data protection and privacy authorities. See https://globalprivacyassembly.org/.

[3] Reports available from https://www.hiqa.ie/reports-and-publications/health-information.

[4] The ten national health care datasets included in this study were hospital in-patient data, mental hospital in-patient data, emergency care data, primary care data, prescription medicines data, cancer registry data, diabetes registry data, CVD registry data, mortality data and long-term care data.

[5] Hospital inpatient data and population health survey of the National Center for Health Statistics (NCHS) are regularly linked to Centers for Medicare & Medicaid Services (CMS) data, Medicare Beneficiaries Summary File (MBSF) and the National Death Index (NDI). Prescription medicines data are linked to Centers for Medicare & Medicaid Services (CMS) data, the National Death Index (NDI), Housing and Urban Development (HUD) data, Social Security Administration (SSA) data and the United States Renal Data System (USRDS) data. See Oderkirk (2021[10]).

www.ingramcontent.com/pod-product-compliance
Lightning Source LLC
Chambersburg PA
CBHW080339270326
41927CB00014B/3295